Oil for Your Lantern

Sharing Light After the Death of a Child

Elizabeth Brady

SCRIPTORIA

an imprint of Sunbury Press, Inc.
Mechanicsburg, PA USA

an imprint of Sunbury Press, Inc.
Mechanicsburg, PA USA

For information about special discounts for bulk purchases, please contact Sunbury Press Orders Dept. at (855) 338-8359 or orders@sunburypress.com.

To request one of our authors for speaking engagements or book signings, please contact Sunbury Press Publicity Dept. at publicity@sunburypress.com.

FIRST SCRIPTORIA PRESS EDITION: November 2024

Set in Adobe Garamond | Interior design by Crystal Devine | Cover by Victoria Mitchell | Edited by Sarah Peachey.

Publisher's Cataloging-in-Publication Data
Names: Brady, Elizabeth, author.
Title: Oil for your lantern : sharing light after the death of a child / Elizabeth Brady.
Description: First trade paperback edition. | Mechanicsburg, PA : Scriptoria Press, 2024.
Summary: We live in a grief-illiterate society. After the death of a child we often hear "there are no words." But there are words. *Oil for Your Lantern* offers the newly bereaved, and those who love them, a gentle introduction to life after the death of a child, sharing words when we don't yet have them ourselves. Elizabeth Brady's essays explore practical, cultural, and spiritual aspects of mourning a beloved child.
Identifiers: ISBN : 979-8-88819-248-1 (paperback).
Subjects: SELF-HELP / Death, Grief, Bereavement | FAMILY & RELATIONSHIPS / Death, Grief, Bereavement | RELIGION / Christian Living / Women's Interests.

Designed in the USA
0 1 1 2 3 5 8 13 21 34 55

For the Love of Books!

Contents

Part III

An Opening

Mack was here and then he was gone. A whole part of me was severed. After years of constant love, daily care, laughter, energy, how does one survive such an amputation?

Our son, Mack, died suddenly of a blood infection on New Year's Eve 2012. He was two weeks shy of his ninth birthday. My husband, Christian, our fifteen-year-old daughter, Izzy, and I were surrounded by family and friends who shared our shock and broken hearts.

In the days after Mack died, there was tremendous energy uplifting us. We heard from friends and family far and wide who came to be with us, and others who reached out on social media to share their sorrow. Somehow, we managed to address the practical demands of the funeral home arrangements, obituary, coffin selection, burial plots, and church service details.

When I read that the banquet of heaven will feel more like a wake than a wedding, it felt right to me. Upon reflection, I think it's because there is a refreshing authenticity in the wake of death when difficult relationships are softened and old hurts melt away for a time. Perhaps it is a glimpse of our own homecoming, when all the crooked places will be made straight.

But there are also excruciatingly quiet moments.

These first days and hours of loneliness were a foretaste of life in the months beyond death. The casserole train eventually ends, energy and relationships that expanded for a time contract, and time trudges on whether or not we are prepared for it.

In the nights after Mack died, I lay in my spot on the left side of the bed, on my left side. I had cried so many tears they had dried up. One night, I was exhausted, dozing, regarding the winter moonlight streaming into the room underneath the shade.

"Mom. Mom!" Mack roused me. I heard him clearly. More than ten years later, as I write this, I can recall this moment, his voice. It is seared into my memory. I opened my eyes widely to listen.

"Yes, I'm here," I answered, not out loud, but clearly inside.

"Tell Z," he said.

Z was a friend of his who was special to him. Z knew Mack had died, and I sensed he wanted me to assure Z of his love.

"I will," I said.

I lay there for a long time, every hair on my body alert.

"I love you, Mack."

He said nothing more directly to me that night, but I was strangely, deeply, comforted by a certain knowledge of his familiar presence.

The next morning, I got up early, filled my mug with coffee, and sat at my desk. I had formed a practice of morning prayer, reading, and writing in my journal as a short-term missionary in West Africa many years earlier. Time and spaciousness in the quiet hours continue to be my life's single most nourishing habits.

But that morning was different. After Mack spoke to me, I knew he was still there and that the bridge to him was within my soul. What had always been an enjoyable morning ritual of peaceful reflection became a lifeline.

I said out loud: "God, I am knocking, loudly, on your door. I know I can't follow Mack, but I hear him, I feel his presence, I sense his love. I want to know more. I want to understand. I don't want to be afraid of my own life. Help me to enter in. Help me."

My choice to keep the door to my soul open reflects my daily quest to fully embrace my whole life. My decision to stay open acknowledges the paradox of life that lies in plain sight—the one the mystics have written about for hundreds of years. Yet I don't think we see until we can't see anything else.

The paradox is that living with the death of Mack and the lives and loves of my husband and daughter is a constant wrestling match. It is learning to hold love, despair, hope, anger, courage, faith, and doubt, all at the same time. It is reconciling death as part of life.

Over the years, I have written my way toward greater clarity and a deepening understanding of living with Mack's death. I am still learning.

The first section of this book is essays I wrote in the early months and years after Mack died. I have kept them true to my experience at that time as we painfully learned to live without him. The second section walks through the calendar of holidays each year and how we continue to include Mack in our family. The third section shifts to the interior journey and the inexhaustible garden of growth that is ours to cultivate.

I am a Christian, and write through the lens of an active faith. I have found great wisdom and practical help in the contemplative writers of old and new. As an Episcopalian, I write through the seasons and celebrations of the liturgical calendar. I have no spiritual agenda other than to share how, after Mack's death, I was abruptly tossed through a threshold into a disorienting new terrain that I am still finding my way to be in.

When I first began reading and actively engaging with the writings and the communities of bereaved parents, I was frankly exhausted by the idea that bereavement is measured in decades. The fact that grief enters your whole remaining life flies in the face of our consumer culture that urges us to fix, numb, or ignore the pain of death. The truth is, the death of our loves is something we learn to carry throughout our own remaining lives. It is endless, as is our love for them and their love for us.

I think of this collection of essays as sharing a pot of oil to help light your lantern along the path ahead. We must all learn to carry our own lanterns, but sharing our oil helps lessen the shadows.

If you are reading this book you have likely been unwillingly initiated into this club of the bereaved. I think you will find, as I have, that some of the most passionate lovers of life give endlessly because of, and not in spite of, the death of their own loves.

Elizabeth, 2024

PROLOGUE
The Longest Night

This is an audio transcript shared with permission from an interview my husband, Christian, and I did with Bill Littlefield of the Only a Game radio program produced by WBUR, Boston.[1] It aired June 23, 2017, five years after Mack's death. Christian was a big fan of the show, so he pitched Mack's story and we were invited on the air.

Bill Littlefield also interviewed a couple teammates of Mack's and the former coach of Penn State men's soccer. I think it presents a wide lens of the way in which his teammates continued to carry Mack with them and the unfolding legacy of the Mack Brady Soccer Fund.

Transcript begins with Quinn Murphy, one of Mack's best friends and teammates.

"I mean, if you have Mack in goal, like, you gotta work hard still," Quinn Murphy says. "But you can trust him that he's yelling at you to get in the right position, and making sure your team doesn't give up easy goals."

Murphy, a thirteen-year-old soccer player, knows the value of a good goalkeeper.

So did Vladimir Nabokov. He once wrote: "The goalkeeper is the lone eagle, the last defender. Less the keeper of a goal than the keeper of our dreams."

Nabokov didn't have Mack Brady in mind. Not literally, at least. He was dead long before Mack was born. But hold what Mr. Nabokov said in mind anyway, okay? Humor me.

Anyway, according to Mack's mother, Elizabeth Brady, the love of soccer came early to her son.

"I Will Stay"

"He has an older sister, Izzy, who is about six years older than he is," Elizabeth says. "And we were actually taking Izzy to a soccer summer camp, but he was too young. And when we got there, Izzy decided, 'I'm not sure this is for me.' And he was standing there in the midst of the soccer camp, and I think he was probably two, and he was, like, 'I will stay. I will stay! I'll go in her place!'

"This is something he loved. And he would be in the backyard with his soccer ball, and he always had his ball with him. So we just went with his energy."

Mack's energy sometimes complicated things for his family . . . such as when everybody was expected at a wedding that conflicted with the schedule of the State College Celtics . . . the youth soccer team in Pennsylvania for which Mack, then seven, was playing.

"Suddenly you're, like, 'Is soccer taking over our lives?'" asks Elizabeth. "'Shouldn't he be at the family wedding?' And yet he was so sincere about needing to be in Pittsburgh with his team. I wrestled with this for a couple of weeks, and Mack would come up to me and say, 'So have you made a decision yet? I need to be with my team.'

"We said, 'Okay. You go.' And he car-pooled with one of the other family teams. And we were at the wedding, and then we were at the reception, getting text after text, play-by-play of what was happening. And Mack just emerged that day, just came into his own, I think. And we've often mused on the fact that we weren't there. But we honored him."

"And, of course, thanks to contemporary technology, you were sort of there because your phone kept pinging," I [Bill] joke.

"Absolutely. We were the annoying relatives at the reception with our phones under the table," Elizabeth says.

The Last Line of Defense

Mack didn't just love soccer. Unlike almost every other small child crazy about that game, Mack fell in love with goaltending. His dad, Christian Brady, a former water polo goalie, was pleased.

"He tried it out one day, and I tried my best and failed many times to be a quiet parent on the sidelines. But at home we would work a little bit on angles and mindset," Christian says. "I would talk with him, you know, five or six years old, 'Only worry about the balls in front of you. Don't worry about the balls behind you,' and so forth. And for whatever reason, he liked being responsible for the defense of his goal. He liked being back there for his teammates. I once taught him to tell your players where the ball is. Tell them to cover the weak side. And the next thing I know, in the game you hear, 'Weak! Weak! Weak!'"

Christian and Mack went to lots of Penn State soccer games together. There, Mack studied goalkeeping at the college level.

"It always amazed me, actually, how . . . the very next game he would play, I would see something that one of our Penn State keepers had done, that Mack was now incorporating in his own play," Christian says. "Which is remarkable because, half the time, I'd be watching the game intently, and he'd be talking with his buddies or doing something else. But he was clearly paying attention at some point."

According to one of Mack's teammates, John Cobes, "clutch" didn't begin to describe Mack's play. Cobes says Mack could be funny, even goofy, but "every time you needed a save, it just didn't get past him."

Mack's plan was to play one day at Penn State. Excellence there would put him on the U.S. National Team's radar, and he hoped he'd also gain the attention of his favorite pro team, Real Madrid. Childhood is for dreaming.

Striking A Match

In the aftermath of Christmas 2012, it all seemed possible for an eight-year-old goalkeeper.

And then, after a day of sledding and playing in the snow, Mack started to run a fever. Neither of his parents thought it was serious. One of Mack's pals had some flu symptoms and recovered overnight. But Elizabeth and Christian called the doctor, just to be safe.

"So they said just call back in the morning if he still has a fever," Christian says. "So, 7:30–8:00

in the morning, on New Year's Eve morning, I called them and they said, 'Okay, bring him in at 4:30 this afternoon.' So then I took him into the doctors, and in hindsight I realized that the first physician there, he clearly realized something more was wrong. And, um, Bill, I'll do my best on the details here.

"Within about forty-five minutes, he said, 'You really need to take Mack to the ER. . . . So they bring him into the ER. You know, they didn't really know what was going on. They were trying to do blood work and so forth, and after a few hours they said, 'There's just not much that we can do here. We need to Life Flight him to a hospital.' So they bundled him up on the stretcher, and the helicopter crew came and got him. And we prayed with him, and we stood outside and watched the helicopter take off. I took a video, because I knew he'd want to see the helicopter he'd been in."

Mack never would see the video. He died in the helicopter as his parents were driving from State College to Hershey.

"When he wasn't in the intensive care unit, I had a hunch that things weren't good," Christian says. "And the chaplain came and met us and took us down to the quiet room. And I told

Elizabeth, I said, 'He's gone.' And she said, 'How do you know?' And I'm trained as an Episcopal priest and ordained, and I said, 'They don't bring the chaplain to the quiet room when things are going well.'"

Sepsis had shut down Mack's organs so quickly that even the doctors who saw him in State College had no chance to save him. Christian remembered later that one doctor had told him that it could be like somebody striking a match in a dry forest.

Once she'd absorbed the initial shock, Elizabeth Brady began thinking about Mack's fifteen-year-old sister, who'd stayed home while her parents had made the drive to Hershey.

"I said to the chaplain, 'What do I do? Do I call Izzy? Or . . . what do I do?'" Elizabeth says. "And she said, 'No. Go to her.'"

"So we went to her friend's house and banged on the doors. Everyone was sleeping. And finally, her friend's father came down and answered the door, and we said, 'I'm sorry to wake you, but we just need to get Izzy.' So we were able to rouse her and bring her down and tell her in person. And I think about that because, later, she remembered that. That was important to her, you know."

Mack's Legacy

With Izzy, Christian and Elizabeth mourned Mack's death. Then, almost without a pause, they celebrated his life. They were determined to help Mack's teammates deal with the loss of their pal . . . their goalkeeper.

Penn State coach Bob Warming remembers hearing Christian's concerns about the kids.

"A lot of them, obviously, were very sad and shocked in some ways," Warming says. "And some of them thought they didn't know if they wanted to play soccer again, just because they associated soccer with Mack."

Christian Brady's concern led to the creation of an annual clinic for Mack's teammates and other soccer players in the community. Members of the Penn State varsity and a couple of players who'd graduated—one of whom was playing professional soccer—staged a day to celebrate Mack and his love for the game.

"Well, the very first clinic was only, gosh, not even two weeks after Mack died," Elizabeth says. "And I think, initially, there's such an energy to be there. And there was some comfort in coming together and seeing the boys out there playing. And, of course, Mack should have been there. I mean, it's so poignant all the time. But I think that's kind of the flip side, and always the 'both/ and' is that, being isolated from that or stepping away from something that Mack loved, I don't think that would have been healthy for anyone. And so I think by emerging and kind of embracing and stepping back into the energy of it all was healing. Certainly for us but, I think, healing for everybody."

The Brady family established a fund to benefit the recruiting and training of future goalkeepers at Penn State. And the Penn State team decided that one game each year should be designated "The Mack Brady Game." As it happens, Penn State has never lost the Mack Brady Game . . . and from time to time, that game has featured an inexplicable moment . . . at least according to Christian Brady.

"Year before last, I'm pretty sure it was Indiana that we played. We were about fourteen minutes in. And of course, it was a horrible call—a penalty kick—because it was against my team," Christian explains. "We thought, 'This is not a good start.' Matt Bersano was in the goal for us. And, they get on the line, player comes up to the spot, Matt dives to the left, gets his left hand on the ball, blocks it. And they win 1–0 by the end of the game. I think that was the final score.

"And Coach Warming . . . he turned around after that penalty stop and hugged me so tight I lost all breath. And he said, 'Mack, that's all Mack.' That's a—that's a pretty good feeling, isn't it?"

Thanks to the love and determination of Mack's parents, and of the various people, young and old, whom he touched during his short life, all sorts of grand and surprising things have come about in the wake of that life.

And Elizabeth Brady has found in these positive developments a capacity for serenity.

"I would much rather be standing on the sidelines, bundled up in a sweatshirt, watching Mack, you know," Elizabeth says. "But, that wasn't our choice . . . so . . . Mack's legacy, in a sense, with his friends and everything, is one of energy and pride and excitement—instead of our grief. As it should be."

Elizabeth Brady doesn't deny the grief. "We will always be the parents of two children," she tells me. She's not someone who feels one can "get over" the death of a child. "You learn to carry it," she says. And in creating ways to sustain the enthusiasm they treasured in their son, and to celebrate their love for him to the benefit of many others, she and her family have carried it, and they've done so much more.

Part I

Just Me and Mack, the Morning Shift

I have read that "morning person" is an inherited gene. I definitely received it from my father. C and Iz are *not* morning people. As Mack got older, it became apparent that he had inherited the gene, and we would often share the "morning shift," as I called it.

Each morning, I slip downstairs in the predawn hours to write in my journal, to pray and think with a fresh cup of coffee and glorious, complete silence. I developed the habit in the early nineties while on the mission field in Burkina Faso, and I have continued to cherish the quiet hours throughout my adult life. I have filled a bookshelf of handwritten journals, but I began to type my reflections in a Word document after Iz was born in 1997.

My desk is in what we call the playroom. It is a garage-size open space with workstations and toys and a stairway up to the loft where Mack kept his Legos intact. My desk sits at an east-facing window that opens onto the backyard. Each morning, the sunrise peeks through the trees; some mornings, rain pelts the window, while other days bring a brilliant display of orange and purple, but the sun is always there. I am still here, too, at the same desk, in front of the same window that Mack would throw snowballs at to get my attention, or where I would watch him drag limbs across the yard to build his teepee on the side of the house.

There are particular spaces I share with Mack, uniquely ours, and the morning shift was one of those. Those spaces are where I feel the sharp stab in my gut that he has died, the true and deep loss of his physical presence. I have had moments when I bend over in pain and catch my breath because of the cut to my soul.

In the early days after Mack's death, after I heard from him so directly, I returned to my desk and would sit with my coffee and stare numbly at the sunrise and think about Mack. I knew this was the space where I would find him.

Who is taking care of you? I would ask. *That is my job.* And I loved it.

With warm familiarity, I can recall many mornings I would emerge from the bathroom and find him sitting at the top of the stairs in the dark.

"Mack?" I would ask.

"I just wanted to be the first downstairs!" and he would sprint down the stairs. "Beat ya! Ha ha!" Then he'd run off.

On other days, I would come down in the dark to find him snuggled into his favorite chair, watching the British television series *Midsomer Murders*, of which he was an unlikely devotee.

A few days before Christmas 2012, I walked toward my desk in the playroom with my coffee, assuming he was still in bed. A small light caught my eye, and I smiled when I discovered Mack in the dark playroom, the only light coming from his Lego headlamp. The yellow headband forced his hair to stand at attention, the Lego figurine shining a small LED light onto the table. I leaned against the doorway and watched him.

He had pulled on his blue fuzzy robe. It was untied and draped on the floor around the little wooden chair he sat in at the matching table where he built his Legos. He was hunched over his latest—an early Christmas gift from his grandparents—a Ferrari. He had placed the numbered plastic bags in a tidy arc on the floor.

"What?" he said without looking up, a little smile at the corner of his mouth. He knew I was charmed by his ways.

"Do you want some juice?"

"Sure," he said.

I got his juice and sat at my computer as he quietly finished his project at his work table behind me. No fanfare. No fuss. His Lego head-lamp, in his robe, in the dark, up before me, diligently working in the pre-dawn hours. A beautiful person.

Each morning, I come to this same space. After hearing from Mack on that night shortly after he died, I knew my connection to him was through my soul. Several mornings in the months after Mack died, I distinctly remember saying out loud, "God, I am still here. I am here. I am here. I am knocking loudly on your door to find Mack, to find my way, to find you. Help me."

I came to meet God. I came to meet Mack. It is in these shared spaces that I slowly understood that he still *is*. And, I chose to embrace the mystery I felt but did not fully comprehend—how Mack died, yet my love for him and his love for me did not.

The Downstairs Thief

I had a vivid dream shortly after Mack died. I walked into our house through the front door and immediately realized we had been robbed. I made my way tentatively through each familiar room, surveying overturned furniture, shattered lamps. I noted the computers were taken, and the silver.

But something inside assured me that they didn't make it upstairs.

On New Year's Eve 2012, we canceled our plans because Mack had what we thought was the flu, and we were looking forward to a quiet evening by the fire. We did not know, and we will never know, why or how an infection entered the bloodstream of our athletic, vibrant, almost nine-year-old son and stole his life in a matter of hours. I had never heard of "sepsis" before Mack died and did not know that it is a silent killer who arrives, like a thief.

When I had this dream, it seemed obvious to me that we had been robbed of a beautiful person in our lives, and the joy of watching Mack grow and continue to achieve his dreams. It wasn't until later, as I began to learn to live with the loss of Mack, that I came to appreciate that the thieves did not make it upstairs.

Our upstairs is intimate. In our home, built in the 1970s, the four bedrooms are separated by a narrow hallway, carpeted down the middle, making it cozy and warmer than the rest of the house.

My husband traveled frequently, so the kids and I would often head upstairs early and take our showers, put on our jammies, and snuggle together in our king-sized bed to read or watch *The Voice* when it was in season.

It is an intoxicating feeling, one I can close my eyes and recall with ease: my arms around each of them, their heads resting on my shoulders, Mack's hair tickling my nose, Izzy smelling like baby powder, so safe and warm and peaceful.

On that afternoon of New Year's Eve 2012, I scooped Mack into my arms and carried him upstairs for a bath before his dad took him to the doctor's office.

"My Romeo," I said to him, then kissed him, bathed him, and dressed him in his favorite

D.C. United sweatshirt, an everyday act that now seems sacred.

I have learned that death doesn't rob us of everything. Some areas of ourselves are untouchable, even to death.

The upstairs of life remains. My love for our children, our most intimate moments of care: bath, bedtime stories, prayers, nights of sickness, hurtful days at school, hiding treats and notes under their pillows, sneaking in to watch them when they sleep. All these remain.

Death stole none of these; the memories have come into sharp relief as unreachable treasures outside of death's grasp. Love is stronger than death, and this awareness has empowered me.

Death is a downstairs thief.

A Return to Daily Living

I copied this reflection from a journal entry written on January 14, 2013, two weeks after Mack died but two days before his ninth birthday, January 16. Mack always enjoyed grocery shopping with me. I share it here because it captures the disorienting nature of sudden death.

Before Izzy got home from school, I drove to the grocery store and realized I hadn't been there in ten days or so, which must be a record. I am normally there almost every day.

I skipped the glazed-donut-Mack-bribery section, as we called it, but I smiled as I walked past because I could see you put your hands under your face like an angel and bat your eyelashes to convince me to let you have a donut. I always did, but I liked your antics.

I headed into the seasonal section. You would have wanted every Valentine you saw, tossing treats for this teacher and that coach into the cart. I spotted a little brown stuffed monkey with a pink embroidered kiss on its cheek. I put it in the cart, because it reminded me of you. You were always irritated with me for getting lipstick on your cheek, but you loved to be loved, so goofy and loving.

Then, I continued through the dairy section to pick up a block of butter when I saw the display of Pirate's Booty puffed cheese twenty-four-count boxes. I stopped. I recalled last year and how, when we saw it, you insisted on taking it in for the whole class as your birthday treat. We bought two boxes of individual bags, and you laughed all day at the name Pirate's Booty. You couldn't wait to take it to school and laugh with John and your friends. It was a hit, and we bought it all season. Of course, you called it Boo-T and made this ahoy-matey pirate gesture every time you opened a bag, which made Izzy laugh.

I stood in front of the tower of Boo-T for a while.

When I eventually came back from my musings, I realized I had only the stuffed monkey and one lonely block of Irish butter in my cart! I glanced at my phone and noticed I had been at the store for over half an hour, clearly walking around in a daze. I pulled my list from my purse to gather my thoughts.

Suddenly, so clearly, I was reminded of our discussion in December about having your birthday snack day on Tuesday before John left for Florida. "The boxes are right there! Get it!" You would've run over and picked it up and thrown it in the cart. I put down my list and picked up the twenty-four-count box of Booty cheese puffs for your class.

I finished my shopping and wheeled toward the checkout when you again reminded me:

"Kuchen! You forgot the raspberry kuchen for my birthday breakfast!" I wheeled back through the bakery section and picked up your favorite breakfast coffee cake to continue the tradition my mom started. She'd gather all of us together in the pre-dawn hours to start our birthdays with presents and treats. My siblings and I have continued the tradition with our own families.

I laughed and chuckled the whole way home. I felt you, and it felt good. These moments when I sense you near are fragile, like a butterfly that lands on your arm—if you move too fast or try to grasp too tightly, it flutters away.

So I listen. I am quiet. A new relationship with you unfolds within me.

Keep the Door to Your Soul Open

I wrote this essay in December 2017, approaching the fifth holiday season without Mack.

When someone we deeply love dies, to the outside, it looks like war. It is devastation, heartache, and chaos. All of our plans are razed, and life looks barren. It is hard to see beyond the scorched earth, which is why it should not surprise you when random acquaintances catch sight of you at the grocery store and clutch their hearts, shake their heads in sorrow, and say, "I can't imagine losing my child. How are you surviving? I don't think I could."

And in the early months of grief, I wasn't sure myself, and I would respond, "Don't. Because you can't even imagine."

Now that I am approaching the fifth anniversary of Mack's death, I can better appreciate the fear in their question. Those of us who have lived through trauma—quite literally survived, defined as *lived beyond*—need to speak to the unexpected shoots of growth and renewal when life as we know it is razed to the ground.

Elizabeth Lesser describes this survival as being "broken open" in her book of the same title, which touches on death, divorce, job loss, mental health, illness, and all of the sufferings of our human experience.[2]

After Mack died, someone gave me a pocket-sized daily devotional called *Healing After Loss*, written by Martha Whitmore Hickman, who was also a bereaved parent. I carried it in my purse for two years until the binding weakened, the cover fell off, and each page was dotted with notes and stained with my tears.

One of the daily reflections was credited to her own grandmother, who had also lost a child. She encouraged Hickman to "Keep the door to her life open" to her deceased daughter. Hickman understood this to mean, "Not only in the reminiscences from the past, but in the extension of the person's spirit into our ongoing lives."[3]

This notion struck me, and I copied it in my journal. I decided that I, too, would keep the door to Mack's life open. And the door to my soul open to Mack. I had experienced a variety of dreams, visions, and random signs after Mack died that surprised me but also offered unexpected comfort and peace.

Still, these experiences unsettled me.

I arrived at my desk in the early hours and regularly said to God, "I have no idea what is happening, but help me. I don't want to be afraid. I know that Mack is with you and I want to enter in. I want to fully embrace my own experience. I want to fully live my own life."

Quotes from Ranier Maria Rilke were throughout Hickman's book. I resonated with Rilke's observation, "when something new has entered into us, something unknown; our feelings grow mute in shy perplexity, everything in us withdraws, a stillness comes, and the new, which no one knows, stands in the midst of it and is silent."

You won't be surprised to learn that not many people were comfortable talking with me about my sense of a growing relationship with Mack beyond death. It was new territory for me, and I was unsure of myself. I realized I needed to learn from other bereaved parents for insight.

I have met many grieving people who have experienced the unexplainable. Sometimes they share a dream or vision, and their friends or family unwittingly shame or chastise them, so they tuck it away so people don't think they are "weird."

When you sit a group of the bereaved in a room and allow a safe place to share, it becomes abundantly clear that our loved ones are very present in our lives and assure us of their love in a variety of ways.

I have come to think that when Mack died, a part of me died with Mack. A part of me—my heart, my soul—is with Mack, and Mack is still a part of me. The love we share with one another creates this unbreakable bridge between us, between this world and the next.

I think the death of someone we love lights up this bridge in our souls. It is our choice whether or not we are willing to traverse it.

Death cannot break this bridge. In fact, I think death illuminates it.

When I chose to step onto the bridge into unknown territory, I began an unexpected journey in my own life. Meeting death and facing it head-on, I became aware of my finiteness and that of everyone I love. Time is not on my side. I have deepened my prayer life, and I feel awake. Mack's death has given me clarity. I know death does not have the final word. Love is stronger than death.

We should keep the door to our soul open to our loved ones because they are still there. And if we are open to the slow unfolding of this new awareness, it offers us great comfort, mercy, and love.

Don't shut the door of your soul to your loves. When the bridge of love lights up the darkness of your soul, try not to be afraid.

A Keeper

Mack used two soccer cages in the backyard almost every afternoon after school to practice blocking balls.

One afternoon, Mack kicked the ball back to me, hitting me square in the forehead. I bent over in pain and fell on my back, spread-eagle in the grass. Mack ran up and leaned over me. I felt his nose near mine.

"I literally saw stars," I moaned. My head began to clear, and I opened one eyelid to see his teddy bear brown eye near mine.

Mack smiled. "You are a *really* bad player, ya know that?"

I pulled him down on the ground and we wrestled, me tickling him. We both laughed until he wiggled away and hopped up.

"Get up, lady! We have work to do!"

Mack was always ready to go and do. I had stopped questioning why he carried a soccer ball with him no matter where we went. He would tuck the ball under his arm as we got out of the car and say, "In case someone wants to play."

Mack was tall for his age—his dad is tall, so we had an inkling he would also be tall. His legs grew faster than the rest of his body, and when he started running and stretched out his legs, he looked a bit like a gazelle with long, skinny limbs that packed a lot of lean muscle.

"Wow, look at Mack run," one of the moms said out loud, mostly to herself, as we watched from the sidelines of the soccer field. I nodded in agreement. He looked free.

In the late winter of March 2012, Mack and his teammates were finishing up an indoor soccer league in Pittsburgh, where they were tied for first place. They had three games on that Saturday, the same day my husband's niece was getting married in Williamsport.

I mulled for a long time over whether Mack, eight at the time, should come to the family wedding or if we should allow him to carpool with another family to Pittsburgh and join his team.

"Mom, I'm the keeper. I need to be there," he said. "I can't let them down."

We eventually decided to let him go with his team, and Iz, C, and I went to the wedding. On that day, Mack emerged and made some amazing showstopping moves we heard about via texts throughout the day.

I have often reflected on how we weren't there to see his greatest games.

"But you respected him and let him go," my mom encouraged me. "It empowered him."

New Routine for 3:15

The kids' bus stop was at the end of our small cul-de-sac, in view from our living room window. I returned from campus by 3:15 P.M. each day to meet Mack and, later, Iz, when her bus dropped her off at 4 P.M., before the whirlwind of evening activities and homework.

In the early days of January after Mack died, I would stand in the window at 3:15 and watch the bus pull up, the kids run off, but Mack wasn't there. I felt like a woman on the widow's walk of her house, waiting for the ship to return to the harbor, knowing full well it would not.

How often had I watched Mack get off the bus, run across the street, and then slowly walk down the cul-de-sac with his baseball cap pulled tightly on his head and his backpack fastened across the front of his chest? He knew I was watching him and would sometimes break into dance or stick his tongue out for my delight. I would open the garage, and he would walk up, kick off his shoes, hang his hat and backpack, lift his cheek for a kiss, and dive onto the couch.

Our good friend, who happens to be a psychiatrist, visited us for a few days in late January, shortly after Mack's death. He asked me how I was doing, and I shared with him that there were key points in the day where Mack's absence was overwhelming for me: in the early morning, and at 3:15 P.M. when we shared time alone each day.

"Change your routine," he suggested.

Instead of coming home, I offered to pick up Iz when the high school let out at 3:17 P.M. She was pleased to have a warm car waiting for her and to forego the forty-five-minute bus trip!

This change became a new, enjoyable ritual Iz and I kept throughout the rest of high school. I was amazed by how much she shared about her school day, having just walked out the doors instead of enduring the bus ride to detox on the way home.

"I like that you're here for me, Mom," she said one day, the snow swirling as we drove to the coffee shop drive-thru for afternoon beverages.

"Me too, babe," I said casually.

But my mind raced with all kinds of thoughts from Mack's wake, when a friend whispered to me that, when he was Iz's age, his own brother had died, and his parents essentially died as well.

"It was like collateral damage," he said to me. "I lost all of them."

When my phone alarm vibrated in the winter months after Mack died, I would lie there in the dark for an instant before the reality of Mack's death washed over me—again.

"God help me," I said out loud every morning. "Truly, help me. I will not lose one child to death and the other to my grief. Help me be the parent Iz deserves."

I would sit up in bed, then lift one leg at a time to place my feet firmly on the floor and will myself to stand. And every morning, I repeated a little ditty I'd picked up in my reading:

"How do I respond to fear? Face Everything and Rise, or Fear Everything and Run. It is my choice."

Rise. Rise. And rise again.

Marriage After Loss

In the months after Mack died, C moaned in his sleep. It would wake me, and I'd lay there in the dark, tears streaming down my face because I was afraid there was no end to our descent into pain. There was nothing I could do to fix his hurt. I reached out and pressed my hand on his shoulder until he calmed.

Sometimes it was C's turn, and I woke him up, crying out for Mack in a dream. He would squeeze my hand to wake me.

"I'm sorry, babe," he'd say, giving me another squeeze before rolling back over to sleep.

There is a popular urban myth that 90 percent of bereaved couples are in serious marital difficulty within months after the death of their child. A curious statistic that people like to quote to you at the funeral—similar to someone citing divorce rates at your wedding shower with a mouthful of cake.

But the truth is much more nuanced. According to Sandy Fox, author of *Creating a New*

Normal . . . After the Death of a Child, The Compassionate Friends, a national bereavement organization that supports families after the death of a child, commissioned a survey in 2006 to research marriages after loss. It found that only 16 percent of parents divorce after the death of a child, and only four percent said it was because of the death, citing the fact that there had been problems in the marriage long before the child died. The percentage in 2024 is closer to 30 percent, which tracks with the national average.

"Against all odds, many couples have found their marriages grew stronger after the death of their child," Fox wrote.[4]

C and I grieve differently. The same events impact us uniquely. Learning to give one another space for our individual needs and responses was wisdom we received early on from other bereaved parents. We say to one another, "I'm just feeling the feels." This means, "Please allow me the space to feel what I'm feeling without question or judgment."

Rainer Marie Rilke (1875–1926) was an Austrian poet and novelist. His quotes, many from his letters, are sprinkled throughout almost every book and gift card on grief and suffering I have read. He often wrote about paradox and how we learn to carry more than one truth simultaneously. On marriage, Rilke wrote:

> *This is the paradox of love: two infinites*
> *meet two limitations, two infinite needs to*
> *be loved meet two fragile and limited ca-*
> *pacities to love. Only in the ambit of great-*
> *er love do they not consume themselves, but*
> *walk together, each towards a fullness of*
> *which the other is a sign.*

Grief and loss, whether through death, illness, a job, or a myriad of other losses, have a way of revealing our cracks and brokenness. It is overwhelming to learn the new language and wade through the foreign land of grief and bereavement while struggling to maintain jobs and the daily demands of life—on top of this, old wounds and hastily buried issues from the past are made visible. This is why grief work is utterly exhausting.

Rilke reminds us of the great truth of all good relationships: We can't expect another human to fulfill our deepest needs and bind our wounds, or we will suck them dry. There is work that is ours alone to do. Our spouses, friends, and community can support, encourage, and walk alongside us. But ultimately, the source of strength, courage, mercy, and healing is ours to access within. It is quiet, intentional, daily work toward fullness that Rilke describes as the "ambit of greater love."

Sit Still and Uncover Your Eyes

This essay first appeared on "Modern Loss" on August 13, 2015.

"There is no question of getting beyond it," Katherine Mansfield wrote in a 1920 letter in which she reflected on death. "The little boat enters the dark fearful gulf and our only cry is to escape—'put me on land again.' But it's useless. Nobody listens. The shadowy figure rows on. One ought to sit still and uncover one's eyes."[5]

What does it mean to sit still and uncover one's eyes? For me, it has come to mean facing death and choosing life, sometimes several times a day. But it is not facing death as some abstract notion; it is facing Mack's death and choosing to continue to live and love him and our family.

When Mack died suddenly, our community of soccer, church, family, and friends gathered over the next few days—lifting my husband and me and our daughter and carrying us for a time as we all shared the horror of Mack's abrupt death.

But those times are pauses in life when we come together to honor passages: births, graduations, weddings, and death. Our loved ones come alongside us, but none of them can take on our grief any more than they can nurture a marriage for us. They must eventually attend to their own lives, leaving us to face our agonizing new reality.

The passageway of grief is lined with a thousand doors. I've read this description in various places, not attributed to anyone in particular, but I like it. I often picture the long hallway ahead, light sneaking out from underneath the closed doors. In the early weeks after Mack's sudden death, I would stand in this hallway, unsure of what to do. But now, I open the doors and walk in because I always find him there.

One of the doors I frequently open is Room 37 in Penn State Hershey Children's Hospital, where we arrived behind the Lifelink helicopter. The blood infection hit Mack like a bolt of lightning and overtook his kind heart in a matter of hours. His dad and I cared for his body one last time. We sat on either side of him. I swirled Mack's wild hair through my fingers with my left hand and my right hand held C's hands in Mack's, resting on his chest over his Winnie the

Pooh hospital gown. We sobbed over his body until our tears dried up.

"Your baby," C said to me.

"Your buddy," I said to him.

And we stood and held each other over Mack.

We still do.

It is in Room 37 that our dreams for Mack and his vibrant life, as well as the dreams he had for himself, were severed.

But it is also in Room 37 that I was struck silent by Mack's repose. I dabbed my tears and drank in his face, his long, dark eyelashes resting on his cheeks, and the right corner of his mouth turned up into a slight smile. It was a smile I knew well when he was bemused. *What did you see? Who came for you?* I have asked him many times. His smile speaks to the beyond, to the place where I believe I will join him upon my death.

In *Hour of Gold, Hour of Lead*, Anne Morrow Lindbergh wrote that part of the healing process is the growth of a new relationship with the dead. Lindbergh likens the process to gestation—a hidden, quiet journey within that requires me to sit still and keep the door to my spirit open.[6]

I am not afraid to walk into these rooms anymore because each time I allow myself to venture in, I find Mack, whether in a dream, a memory that causes me to burst out in laughter or tears, or even in a nudge to buy or do something for someone he loves. I have learned to accept these moments of grace as the "flecks and nuggets of gold" in grief that Anne Lamott refers to in her book *Traveling Mercies*.[7]

Mack's sudden death still takes my breath away. But by facing the truth of his death and choosing to live and love him and one another, I can embrace my whole life with my eyes uncovered.

Forging a New Path

At each of the significant intersections of our lives, we hear the joys and sorrows of those who have traveled similar paths before us: college, marriage, a new job, the birth of a child, divorce, travel, and illness. We are awash with family lore through stories, pieces of advice, and fears.

John O'Donohue, the late Irish poet and theologian, called these passages in life *thresholds*. Donohue writes, "The threshold is more than a boundary, frontier or limit. It suggests an imminence of crossing. A threshold is a line of deeper change where the one who crosses is transformed. A profound question inevitably opens a new threshold. The question is the place where the unknown becomes articulate in us."[8]

But when we experience something that few people in our immediate families and communities around us have experienced, we find ourselves in a lonely and disorienting terrain where even the language is new.

Few people in my family or community had experienced the death of a young child. The fear of losing a child is the stuff of nightmares, novels, and Hollywood movies. We keep death distant and impersonal, contained in stories to weep over and consume. When death lands on our doorstep or our friends' doorsteps, we have limited, or, at best, dated, language for it because we have so little actual, lived experience of death.

Often the stories people share with us are not their stories, but stories they have heard from others who have experienced the death of a child. They are stories heavy with the tellers' fears—magnified worries of marriages breaking down, siblings embittered, alcoholism, job loss, depression, and suicide.

In the months following Mack's death, I found myself suffocating in the fears of others. I needed to find the voices and stories of those who learned to survive the death of a child. I needed to learn how they did it. I was desperate for fresh air. I was desperate for hope.

I searched until I discovered these people in a couple of key places: in peer-to-peer bereavement groups like The Compassionate Friends, and in books and articles about child loss and grief written by bereaved parents.

After meeting with and reading the work of other bereaved parents, first in a local community group and later through attending The Compassionate Friends' annual national conferences, I felt relief. I learned from other bereaved parents how important it was to take ownership in my new role and identity as a bereaved parent as much as we take ownership of other parts of our lives: parenting styles, career choices, marriage, finances, health—each are collective and yet individual experiences. Each of us will learn to live with the death of our child differently. It is as unique to us as our personalities and parenting styles, but we must do the intentional and hard work of finding our way into this new identity.

I attended my first national Compassionate Friends conference in 2017. I will never forget the joy I felt when I picked up my check-in packet. It included a nametag with both my name and Mack's. And, because I was a first-time attendee, Mack's name had a little blue butterfly next to it. What a gift to share Mack's name and include him in the weekend without explanation or apology!

When I returned from the conference, a friend said, "Maybe when you get back to normal you won't need to go to those conferences anymore."

By that time, I could respond and offer insight rather than feel defeated and hurt by his innocent comment.

"There is no going back. I am learning to live my new normal. I am on a new path."

And so are you.

Part II

10

We Learn to Carry Mack with Us

We hosted a college graduation party at our house for our nephew in May 2014, roughly a year and a half after Mack died. My husband's family came, including his ninety-five-year-old great-grandmother and all four grandparents in various levels of physical health. Five generations gathered on our back porch to celebrate.

I sat next to my beautiful sixteen-year-old Izzy, listening to the toasts and thinking that, before too long, she would be graduating high school and heading to college. But our sweet Mack, who died suddenly of sepsis on New Year's Eve 2012, was not there. Mack: hilariously funny, silly, and determined, just two weeks shy of his ninth birthday when he died, is ever present, ever absent to me.

It is a real tension those of us who are bereaved understand. We are keen to celebrate the joys of life with family and friends, and we are all *allowed* to live! But, I have grown another eye that senses another space and time—with Mack, in the eternal.

As I prepared the flowers, organized the buffet table, and filled the pitcher with ice cubes, I sensed Mack's presence. He loved when we entertained. I recalled a sentiment from Martha Whitmore Hickman's book, *Healing After Loss*. "Keep the door to your soul open" to your beloved. During that time, I carried Whitman's book in my purse and read it for a little daily courage. I learned from Whitman to allow these moments, not to dismiss them or explain them away.

I felt Mack's joy and smiled through my tears, remembering how he skipped around the house, complained about having to dress up, filled bowls of Fritos and munched on the extras, and huffed that lighting candles was still the realm of his big sister. I laughed out loud at one point during the day, remembering when he told me guests would be "personally offended" if I served them stuffed grape leaves for appetizers.

I miss you, I whispered out loud to him. *I love you, Mackie.*

Once the last guest left, I was exhausted and had to rest on my bed. My daughter curled up next to me, reading funny stories from Buzzfeed. I chuckled to encourage her to read more, but I really just liked the sound of her voice.

Each fall, as Facebook posts fill up with photos of the first day of the new school year, it is easy for each post to be a poignant reminder that there are no new photos of Mack. Every milestone is an opportunity for self-pity. After I shed some tears, I take back the emotional reins, log off from Facebook for a few days, and center myself again.

Meanwhile, I come to my desk every morning with a cup of coffee and spend time in prayer. I read. I think of Mack. I picture his face, I remember a moment, I laugh, I cry. Then, I ask God to help me choose gratitude for his beautiful self, his beautiful life, for life with my daughter and husband, for this day. And tomorrow, I will be back here at my desk, and I will need to choose gratitude again.

11

Día de los Muertos: Eat, Speak, and Remember

A memory of a moment between me and Mack often bubbles up unbidden. In the early days of mourning, these would wound me as a reminder of what I had lost. However, as the years have unfolded, I have come to relish those moments and even invite them.

Recently, I recalled a night when C and Iz were out. It was just Mack and me for dinner. I lit candles, pulled out the fine china, and we sat at opposite ends of the dining table.

Mack peered around the candles and commented from his end of the table, "Really?"

"I love you!" I giggled.

Remembering that moment again, I say out loud, "I love you, Mack," as I type.

I have come to appreciate that memory lives in a separate space, and at times, Mack and I share a moment. I often laugh out loud and remember Mack's great laugh and feel his warm spirit because we always laughed together.

In Henri Nouwen's *Bread for the Journey*, he writes:

> *It is very important to remember those who have loved us and those we have loved. Remembering them means letting their spirits inspire us in our daily lives. They can become part of our spiritual communities and gently help us as we make decisions on our journeys. Parents, spouses, children, and friends can become true spiritual companions after they have died. Sometimes they can become even more intimate to us after death than when they were with us in life. Remembering the dead is choosing their ongoing companionship.*[9]

After Mack died, I took notice of the Day of the Dead, or *Día de los Muertos*, and its bold, bright depictions of death making their way from Mexico onto our store shelves in central Pennsylvania. Day of the Dead refers to the Catholic (and some protestant church) celebrations around Halloween (October 31), All Saints Day (November 1), and All Souls Day (November 2), or the Day of the Dead.

At first, I thought the images of children dancing with caricatures of death, faces painted as skeletons, happily eating sugar skulls and chicken stew with bones, gathered in candlelit cemeteries, were a bit jarring. I now appreciate that their starkness is a welcome reminder of our mortality: life is brief, death will come to us all, so live!

Now, almost eight Halloweens since Mack was with us, as I stroll through the stores looking at the Halloween décor—endless bloody knives, skulls, bats, gravestones, and the recent emergence of the terrifying clown—it strikes me that, in the United States, we have a culture steeped in images of violent death moments. What these images can't tell is the story of the mysterious and vibrant relationship we can have with our loved ones beyond death.

As I continue learning to live with Mack's death, I have become ever more convinced that we need to give ourselves and our loved ones permission to speak the names of our dead and celebrate their continuing presence in our lives. It does not take long when speaking to others in mourning to learn that they, too, have shared moments, dreams, visions, and other gestures of love from the dead that give them tremendous peace. We

can feel their presence in the smallest moments—
anything from random visits from butterflies and
birds, to discovering things like pennies, feathers, or flowers on our paths. I have heard these
experiences characterized as "signs from heaven"
at Compassionate Friends conferences. These
moments are common among the bereaved, and
most agree that the message is to assure us that our
loved ones are okay and present with us.

"I don't tell anyone in case people think I'm
weird," a friend whispered to me about her brother, Grant, who had died the year before, but she
enjoys his presence and friendly banter during her
morning commute when she is alone in the car.

A student of mine spoke of her high school
classmate's recent death by suicide.

"What is her name?" I asked.

"Susan," she said. "Susan. I haven't said her
name since she died. It feels good to say her
name."

To Susan, Grant, Mack, and all of our loved
ones who have died before us but remain with
us, grow in us like a tree: May we invite them to
bear fruit and provide shade to our souls in the
most surprising ways as we enter into a season of
remembrance.

12

An Empty Seat at Thanksgiving

Thanksgiving was the first major holiday after Mack died when we gathered with extended family. We trade Thanksgiving each year between my family and my husband's family, and in 2013, the year after Mack died, it happened to be with my family. I am the eldest of four children, and with my parents, our spouses, and nine grandchildren at that time, we decided to pitch in to rent a house at the beach so we could all stay together. I was relieved not to be at home that first Thanksgiving.

I asked my local bereaved parent group how they managed Thanksgiving. One seasoned bereaved mom said something I have never forgotten: "You don't stop being Mack's mom. You are Izzy and Mack's mom," she said. "I made the mistake of waiting for permission or waiting for others to remember my daughter. That does not happen. If you want Mack to be included, you need to plan ahead and make it happen. And balloons work well."

I emailed my family to let them know we wanted to include Mack, and suggested balloons would be fun and not too heavy, especially for his cousins. "Just tell us what you want us to do," was the collective response. This was new territory for everyone.

I bought biodegradable balloons, a helium tank, colorful string, and non-permanent Sharpies and packed them in the car for the trip. We set out the balloons and Sharpies Thanksgiving morning and invited everyone to write notes to Mack on the balloons before we blew them up. Mack's younger cousins couldn't write yet, but they drew pictures of Mack playing soccer adorned with hearts and soccer balls. We tied the bouquet of balloons to the back of a chair at the dinner table. It was a surprisingly poignant collection of color, drawings, words, and images that allowed space for even the youngest cousin to participate. After dinner, we each released our balloons into the evening sky. It was magical.

When the football game came on and everyone relaxed after a full day, C and I went to our room to lay down. We held each other and cried. We cried because it will never be right that Mack is absent from the Thanksgiving table. And he is ever-present at the family table.

13

Advent: A Visit in the Darkest Hours

During the Advent season of 2003, I was eight months pregnant with Mack. Iz had just turned six and was dressed as an angel, having participated in our church's Christmas Eve children's pageant. She leaned against me, drawing on a notepad, the gold tinsel from her halo tickling my nose, and we smiled at each other when Mack moved and she could feel him through my dress.

"That is so weird, Mama!" she giggled.

There is no way we could have known in that magical season of 2003, in anticipation of Mack's birth in January, that he would die suddenly nine years later on New Year's Eve 2012.

Celebrated during the four weeks between Thanksgiving and Christmas, Advent is a time set apart for us to face the dark places in our own lives and the world. In the liturgical calendar, these four weeks mark a time of preparation not only for the birth of Jesus, but for his long-awaited *second* coming. It is a reminder that Jesus promises to return again and to defeat death once and for all. This is the comfort that no human can offer, and it is the grist of hope. A hope that assures me beyond any human understanding that I will see my son again. But until that time, Advent asks us to keep showing up to life, to be present not just in the joy, but in the pain for one another.

"All of us who take on the risk of mothering take on the risk of living, and dying, because the two are inseparable," wrote Brother David Steindl Rast.

When I sit in Christmas Eve services now and watch the bustle of young families preparing for the children's pageant, I am grateful for the years of busy sweetness when Iz and Mack were young. I smile through my tears, remembering Mack in the children's pageant in his preferred role as an animal. For many years, he was a sheep until he was promoted to donkey and proclaimed to me in his costume, ears askew, "Mom! I'm an ass!"

We laughed together then, and I laugh now and feel his warm and joyful spirit wash over me.

I have thought a lot about Mary and her consent to become the mother of Jesus. Her response to the archangel Gabriel, "Let it be," was just the beginning. Mary's story unfolded far beyond the stable throughout Jesus's life, death, and resurrection. As a bereaved mom, I turned to Mary with new eyes and released her from the confines of an annual pageant scene in a barn. I realized my narrow view of her was a fundamental silencing of a brave and faithful woman from whom I could learn much.

One can only imagine the judgment and gossip swirling around Mary when she was first pregnant. No doubt she left town for some relief to stay with her older cousin, Elizabeth, who was six months pregnant with Jesus's cousin, John the Baptist. I have an icon on my writing desk that C gave me called "The Visitation," which depicts this meeting of the two women. When I ponder the significance of that friendship, I am reminded of the great women in my own life. I think especially of my friend, Eve.

Eve is also a bereaved mom. Our sons were best friends, and she loves Mack and misses him, too. She came to my house every evening throughout the frigid winter of 2013, and we would bundle up and walk the two-mile loop around our neighborhood in the sub-freezing cold while I cried sloppy tears and shared my latest dream, reading, or thought about Mack. She visits Mack's gravesite, where she leaves crosses in the spring and pumpkins during the fall. When I visit his site, I know she has been there. I take a photo and text it to her, thanking her for her love for us.

Eve's steadfast presence taught me not to be afraid of the dark times of others. We don't need to say or fix anything. Some things are broken, and they hurt and need to be acknowledged. We are called to show up, as awkward and imperfect as it feels, to assure each other that we are not alone.

In 2019, the daughter of a good friend died suddenly in a horseback-riding accident. A courageous and passionate young life again cut too soon, leaving the family in stunned shock as they learned to live in their new, painful reality. My friend and her husband received a stack of bereavement books, including one from me, that were piled on her hearth.

"What helps you most right now?" I asked her.

"Nothing really helps," she said. "Except when my friends come to be with me."

Sister Joan Chittister of the Benedictine Sisters of Erie speaks to our moments of deep grief and loneliness: "Have you never been imprisoned by your fears, your embarrassments, your humiliations, your inadequacies?" Sister Joan wrote, "Because if you have, you know that only those who visit you can make a difference."

14

Limp Stockings and Empty Chairs

The holiday season after a loved one dies is exhausting. It is exhausting because the poignancy of each ornament, stocking, favorite dessert, carol, and Christmas tree farm outing crystallizes the pain of their absence and their continued presence in relentlessly concrete, visible ways from Halloween through the New Year.

How we lean into this tension, honoring their presence and grieving their absence, is the ongoing, organic, and, at times, sloppy, endless work of the bereaved. It is not easy to do.

As my family and I approach the tenth holiday season without our son, Mack, I would like to share a few practices that seem to help each of us, though in different ways.

We have heard it a million times: everyone grieves differently. This is true, and it is annoying.

It is annoying because I have had to learn to be patient with my husband in ways that I would never have before Mack died. And, of course, he with me. The same moments indeed hit us differently, and it still surprises me. We have learned to give one another space. "I'm just feeling the feels," we say to one another to give permission to feel what the other may not feel without question or judgment.

During Christmas of 2013, the first after Mack died, we continued our tradition of cutting a fresh tree and putting it up in the family room. While C and Iz wrestled with the tree lights, I hung the stockings above the fireplace and decorated the mantel.

Tucked inside Mack's stocking was a miniature stocking for Fiona, his dwarf hamster. Mack had written "Fi-Fi," her nickname, in marker across the top of the mini stocking and drawn a picture of her as well as he could with a Sharpie.

"That's supposed to be Fi-Fi," Mack explained when he hung it during the Christmas of 2012.

"I got it." I smiled then and smiled again as I hung Fiona's small stocking on the same hook as Mack's and felt him near.

C came up behind me and whispered in my ear. "Mack's stocking looks so sad. It's so empty," he said with tears. "It pains me."

"It pains me, too," I nodded. "But I don't know how to do this any other way. Iz deserves the best of us."

When my friend shared that his brother died as a child, he also noted that his parents essentially died as well. "I lost all of them," he said, "even though my parents were still there." His comment pierced me, stuck with me, and I determined not to lose both children, one to death and the other to my grief. C and I had spoken of this many times. I didn't need to say it again. He knew.

"I know, I know. I agree. I just hurt," he said.

We still hang Mack and Fiona's stockings alongside ours. And so that it doesn't look limp, we encouraged one another to drop mini Legos, Swedish Fish, or fun gifts that remind us of Mack into his stocking throughout the month. Then, on Christmas Day, Iz volunteers to open Mack's stocking, and we delight in the little surprises and trinkets that have made their way into his stocking throughout the month. Somehow the visible gifts are an invitation for his joyful presence to be with us.

If your child, your parent, or another loved one has died, and this is the first holiday without them, nothing can prepare you for the feeling of gathering around the familiar dining table with an empty chair. But you can prepare their favorite apple pie.

As awkward as it feels, you want to talk to whoever is hosting ahead of time about how to remember your loved one as you gather for the holidays. You do not want to assume someone else is taking care of it. Or, worse, that everyone arrives at the table and realizes the absence of that person has become a giant presence in the room because no one has acknowledged it!

Think of things like favorite desserts, a special nametag, or a candle as a gentle opening for your loved one to be present with you.

Because Mack was our young son, we could step in as his parents and plan his remembrance at family Thanksgivings, such as with the balloons our family members wrote or drew on at the beach. Tying them to the back of the chair was a way to include Mack and allow space to speak of him in a light-hearted way.

Since that first year without Mack, I still send notes to my parents and each of my siblings to share holiday memorial plans so that everyone is aware and there are no surprises. The whole family is supportive —"just tell us what you want us to do!" has been the response. Now, remembering

Mack has become a part of the Thanksgiving tradition, even for the younger cousins he never met in person. We offer the opportunity and materials, but participation is not required, and not everyone does.

It is hard but important to remember that grief is as unique to each person as their personality. Giving permission for each family member to respond, or not, as and when they choose, is a gift of generosity. Everyone at the table has passed through a threshold into a new terrain. Learning how to live into life after the death of someone takes time and many permission slips.

Added to the death of your family member, everyone brings other losses to the table, some known and some unknown to those gathered. It helps for each of us to put the mental abacus away and resist the urge to weigh and measure one another.

Above all, give yourself permission to remember and celebrate your loved one! There may be some members of the family who are strangely silent and disapproving of your ideas. You do not need to wait for permission to remember someone you love.

Bake the pie, light the candle, buy the gift, hang the stocking, make a donation in their name, cry sloppy tears, and laugh out loud at an outrageous card you definitely would have given them were they still here, and buy it anyway!

Truly, truly, love does not die. Their absence is painful *and* their presence is endless love.

15

Nuance in the Season of Toxic Positivity

There is an aching gap in our culture between the projected, edited, ideal life our consumer culture sells and the truth of our human lives. There is no avoiding it. And each year in late August, just after school starts, the Madison Avenue gurus herald the coming of the holiday season.

The truth is, it's not just the marketers. Consumer mentality has seeped its way into every institution and all of us. To see with clarity is considered counter-culture, even though it's just being honest.

In various articles seeking to shed light on the mental health effects of the relentless demand to be coiffed and seasonally appropriate, I've come across the term "toxic positivity." The Psychology Group defines it as "the excessive and ineffective overgeneralization of a happy, optimistic state across all situations. The process of toxic positivity results in the denial, minimization, and invalidation of the authentic human emotional experience."[10]

The church is not immune to this. In many churches, the addition of what are termed Blue Christmas services recognizes the need for authenticity. The services vary, but the common theme is to gather on December 21, the longest night of the year, to offer prayers and light candles in recognition of the heavy stuff we carry: death, relationships, illness, addiction.

I have often considered how refreshing it would be to elevate the Blue Christmas service from the basement on the darkest night into one of the regular Sunday morning Advent services. To be honest with ourselves and our young people that life is a palette of color.

Over the years, I changed our Advent wreath candles to visibly reflect a more nuanced holiday season. I have bought candles from freelance artists on sites like Etsy that include the traditional purple and rose, but are marbled with black and white.

When I share these designs with other bereaved parents they immediately appreciate the mixture of colors that represent the truth of our lives: It is joy *and* sadness; it is light *and* dark.

And this visible representation is an opening that gives permission for all of us to acknowledge both the absence and presence, the joy and sadness, of the season.

As the marbled candles so effortlessly swirl together the colors of the holy season, may we give ourselves and one another permission to feel more than one emotion. We are allowed to grieve those who are so poignantly absent at this time of year. And may we also allow ourselves to relish the gift of those present.

16

New Year's Eve—Again

How do we acknowledge a death day?

The very morning of New Year's Eve 2012, I had written in my journal with my favorite mechanical pencil, reflecting on the past year, and then made tidy lists of goals for 2013. That same journal entry continued twenty-four hours later in rushed handwriting with a blue ballpoint pen when I tried to recount how our world turned upside down in a matter of hours. New Year's Eve will always be Mack's death day.

One of the delicate balances of our new life is not only learning how to acknowledge Mack's death day, but how to celebrate the annual holidays. Mother's Day, Father's Day, first and last days of school, birthdays, Easter, Christmas, Valentine's Day, Groundhog Day . . . you get the picture. The list of celebrations is endless, but how do we celebrate life with Iz and honor Mack as an important and continued member of our family at the same time?

As I continued my mourning journey and read further into grief, I was introduced to the work of Dr. Alan Wolfelt, the director of the Center for Loss & Life Transition. Wolfelt created the widely used "companioning model versus a treating model for mourners." Wolfelt's model advocates a ritual of continuity—in our case, we would continue to recognize Mack as a part of our family and include him in the festivities. Wolfelt wrote:

> *Mourning in our culture isn't always easy. Normal thoughts and feelings connected to loss are typically seen as unnecessary and even shameful. Instead of encouraging mourners to express themselves, our culture's unstated rules would have them avoid their hurt and "be strong." But grief is not a disease. Instead, it is the normal, healthy process of embracing the mystery of the death of someone loved. If mourners see themselves as active participants in their healing, they will experience a renewed sense of meaning and purpose in life.*[11]

The notion of actively participating in and experiencing the mystery of death and the journey of healing energizes me. In practical terms, as each holiday approaches, both C and I buy cards for each other and Iz that we know Mack would've loved or picked out himself. I felt Mack's fun spirit with me when I found a perfect Father's Day card for C with "Dad, you're the best" written inside, which is exactly what Mack often said to C. It was also accompanied by a terrible recording of "You're Unbelievable" which made us all laugh. Mack definitely would've picked that card, Iz said. Buying a gift or a card on behalf of Mack for one another, or for Mack, has come intuitively.

Someone I deeply love is not within arm's reach but a constant presence in my heart, mind, and spirit. I want to better understand what I am experiencing. I think we have begun to more fully understand that our grief is in direct relation to our love: we grieve *because* we love. And love remains.

Dietrich Bonhoeffer (1906–1945) offers some insight in *Letters and Papers from Prison*:

> *There is nothing that can replace the absence of someone dear to us, and one should not even attempt to do so. One must simply*

*hold out and endure it. At first that sounds
very hard, but at the same time it is also a
great comfort. For to the extent the emp-
tiness truly remains unfilled one remains
connected to the other person through it.
It is wrong to say that God fills the empti-
ness. God in no way fills it but much more
leaves it precisely unfilled and thus helps
us preserve—even in pain—the authentic relationship. Furthermore, the more
beautiful and full the remembrances, the
more difficult the separation. But gratitude
transforms the torment of memory into silent joy. One bears what was lovely in the
past not as a thorn but as a precious gift
deep within, a hidden treasure of which
one can always be certain.*[12]

17

Mack Brady Match

The Penn State men's soccer team was ready to open their Big 10 season against Maryland. As the fans arrived at Jeffrey Field, C, Iz, and I lined up beneath the bleachers along with Mack's soccer team, the Celtics. We were there to celebrate the fifth annual Mack Brady Match in 2017.

We laughed with the boys as they jostled each other in line, teasing one another about their varying heights. It had been four years and nine months since Mack was their goalkeeper. It is poignant to be with them, to see how they have grown. They are still playful yet strong, and getting taller all the time. I see Mack in them. Moments of wistfulness wash over me, and I hear myself asking Mack: *How tall would you be now? Would you still be the keeper? Would you still eat banana and Nutella sandwiches for lunch before a match?*

Questions without answers, I know. I have learned over the years that I cannot stay in the rooms of my mind I call "the what ifs." I can visit them, feel them, sit in them, cry in them. Then, I slowly back out and close the door so I can turn and celebrate all that is wonderful in life: loving family, lasting friendships, fall days, exciting sports, warm coffee, and love that never dies.

18

Lent as a Verb, Not a Noun

In Christendom Lent, from the old English *lenc-ten*, which means spring, is the annual season of fasting and penitence for forty days before Easter. The standard preparation for Lent asks us to step away from our busy lives and consider our mortality: *for you were made from dust, and to dust you will return.*

Until Mack died, Lent had been a kind of intrusion into my busy life, a bold reminder that all we see around us is finite.

We who mourn the love and presence of a beloved live with a constant reminder of our mortality because a part of us has already died, and yet part of us remains.

Five months after Mack died, just after Mother's Day, I was asleep when I saw Mack come running toward me: sweaty, smiling, vibrant, alive. I approached him and felt my heart leap from my chest.

"Hi!" I said out loud and woke myself up, reaching for him. I blinked into the dark of night, realizing at once, and again, that he *is*, but not here, with me. I fell back onto my pillow, tears streaming. "Dammit, Lord," was all I could muster.

"I love you, Mack," I whispered into the night. My husband reached out and squeezed my hand. I squeezed back.

"The dead are invisible, not absent." This quote is often attributed to St. Augustine of Hippo (354–430). His son, Adeodatus, died at age sixteen.

While the two words are etymologically unrelated, if I consider the *verb* lent, the simple past tense and past participle of "to lend," I begin to understand the noun "Lent" differently. In some ways, our lives are lent to us for a time.

Certainly being the mother of my children, the steward of precious little lives, allowed to see them grow, is an honor. Mack's life was lent, and while he was here with us, we loved and cherished him every day. The length of his life was not within our control, but I am grateful for his time with us, and I am comforted by the certain knowledge that I will see him again.

All of our lives, in a sense, are lent, and it is healthy to be reminded each year through Lent that we have little control over when or how our lives will end. We can be encouraged, though, that Lent ends with Easter Sunday and the resurrection, which promises the end of all suffering and death. I type the words so easily, but I can scarcely imagine what the end of all suffering and death will be like.

19

Holy Saturday: Come Forth and Live

It is Holy Saturday, the gap between death and resurrection, the day between Good Friday and Easter Sunday. It is the gap in which those of us who have lost loved ones live, one part of ourselves here and one part there. I am reminded of other mothers who have survived, literally "lived beyond," the deaths of their children.

The Sandy Hook Elementary School shooting occurred on December 14, 2012. I remember it well because we paused in horror at the news but quickly moved on in the demands of the busy holiday season. I saw Sandy Hook and the surviving parents and families through a very different lens after Mack died, only seventeen days later.

Many of the Sandy Hook parents and families have come forth in honor of their children to establish legacies, advocate for policies around gun reform or mental health, create an animal sanctuary, write books, and participate in bereavement conferences. Their collective action inspires me—it embodies the truth that we cannot control much of what happens to us in life, but we can control our response.

I thought of this great truth again after reading a commentary from Pope Benedict XVI on Mary Magdalene. I love how Mary Magdalene and the other women show up to care for Jesus's body in the tomb. But the stone had been rolled away, and he was not there.

Pope Benedict XVI reflects on their grief:

Despite the miraculous apparition of two angels sitting in the open tomb "one at the head and one at the feet where the body of Jesus had been," Mary Magdalene remains unmoved, consumed only by her grief. Two times heaven has to ask her (once via the angels, the second time by the risen Lord himself) woman, why are you weeping? She has come to her own fatalistic conclusion about what happened to Christ "they have taken my Lord and I don't know where they laid him" and it is from this pessimism that she must be converted. When the risen Jesus speaks her

name "Mary!" like the people on the day of
Pentecost, she was "cut to the heart." The
risen Christ's command to "stop holding
on" pertains to our preconceptions and our
stubbornness as well. Something greater
than our sorrow is now at work in the
world. It is the reason why, even in our
weeping, we bend over and peer into the
tomb, full of expectation.

There is something more to death than death.
It sounds a bit simple but I have been struck by
it many times since Mack's sudden death. Mack's
journey and his legacy of love and passion continue. I stand in awe as I witness it.

It is strangely comforting to stay in the stink-
ing tomb and confines of my mind where all of
my "what ifs and shoulds" for Mack's life fester. It
is a suffocating place.

Like all who hear the call of Jesus as he stands
outside the tomb of ourselves and calls, "Come
forth," I am afraid. But it is the path to newness
and light.

20

Mother's Day, Everyday

"Do you have children?" is likely the most frequently asked question beyond our name and marital status. In the early months after Mack died, this question surprised me when asked at random receptions or work events.

I would launch into an internal dialogue:

Do I say I have two children? Do I say that I have one child but another that died? Will I burst out in tears if I say Mack's name today? Is that too much information? Can I close my eyes and pretend I'm not here, or would that be too weird?

This hesitation on my part often caused a moment of bemusement for the person who asked a seemingly obvious and uncomplicated question.

Over the years, I now say without hesitation: "Yes, I have two children, our adult daughter, Izzy, and our son, Mack, who died in 2012 when he was almost nine."

I have found this elicits several responses.

"Oh, I'm so sorry. I don't know what to say."

I often assure them, "It's okay. Mack is still my son and a part of our family, so I always include him when people ask about our children."

"Oh. Okay. Well, nice to meet you!" and they walk quickly away. "Quiche awaits!"

Or, someone who has met death in their own life responds:

"Oh, I am so sorry," and they share their grief with me and we enrich each other by sharing our stories.

Sometimes someone will walk away and then circle back around to me later and explain:

"I'm sorry, I didn't know what to say. Your openness about your son took me by surprise," and they share their own loss and how often they don't speak of it or feel allowed to speak.

This is why we must teach and share our experiences. We can help each other update the language and experience of grief in a largely grief-illiterate culture.

As I have become more confident in my new identity as a bereaved mom, I often say: "I hope that my speaking about Mack doesn't make you uncomfortable. Mack is our son and will always be a part of our lives. It is our honor to continue to love and remember him."

These words from Henri Nouwen's *Bread for the Journey*, empowered me. I share a reflection called "Holding the Cup" here with you:

> *We must all hold the cups of our lives. As we grow older and become more fully aware of the many sorrows of life—personal failures, family conflicts, disappointments in work and social life, and the many pains surrounding us on the national and international scene—everything within and around us conspires to make us ignore, avoid, suppress, or simply deny these sorrows. "Look at the sunny side of life and make the best of it," we say to ourselves and hear others say to us. But, when we want to drink the cups of our lives, we need first to hold them, to fully acknowledge what we are living, trusting that by not avoiding but befriending our sorrows, we will discover the true joy we are looking for right in the midst of our sorrows.[13]*

21

About Your Room

This essay first appeared on "Motherwell" on July 21, 2023.

Your blue camo backpack hung on the back of your desk chair with your Pittsburgh Penguins baseball cap on top for eight years. It was as you left it on the last day of school before the Christmas holidays in 2012.

It was September 2020. I was in your room with a mug of dark roast and my phone because we had decided to replace the wall-to-wall carpeting upstairs. The installers were coming the next day, and I was on deadline. Both Dad and Iz were out of town. The task of dismantling your room came to me. In truth, it was probably good to have an excuse to finally tackle it. The air in your room was a little stale.

I smiled while looking around your space, remembering the last time we spring-cleaned your room together. While Dad and Iz were at a retreat for the weekend, we decided to clean out your drawers and rearrange the furniture. You had two large plastic bins of stuffed animals, so I suggested you sort them into two piles: one to give away and one to keep. I opened the window and screen above your desk and said, "Toss the ones you want to give away out the window."

"Are you kiddin' me?" You laughed and peered through the window at the porch below.

"Sure!" I smiled at your delight. "We can collect them off the porch later to give away."

How you laughed! "This is totally awesome," you said, then lobbed a handful of beanie babies out the window.

Your desk was essentially how you left it, except for the absence of Fi-Fi's cage. We had given your dwarf hamster to Mrs. W's classroom a few months after you died. Fi-Fi had been lonely without your attention. She was surprisingly social, and delighted the class until she died a few years later. Mrs. W read the students a book about dealing with the death of a pet, and for some reason, it sent me into a fit of giggles thinking of you and how you would have reacted to all the fuss. They buried Fi-Fi under the tree dedicated to you in front of the school.

Over the years, your bed became a depository of gifts for you. There were several signed professional soccer jerseys. Iz bought you mini snow globes and left them on your nightstand. Dad continued to buy you key chains from his travels. I bought a stuffed animal for every event and holiday that reminded me of you: a monkey with a red kiss on the cheek, a little brown bear with blue slippers, and puppies of all colors and sizes. It was an impressive mountain of animals! As I sifted through the pile, I reread the date and event on each tag that I had the foresight to jot down so I was reminded of the occasion.

Your room remained a place where we came to remember you and leave mementos we would have shared with you. But you were frozen in time in that room as an almost-nine-year-old boy. I had been in many bereaved parent groups when the discussion of "stuff" came up. It can be a source of great tension between couples and families. Long before I met your dad, his grandmother had tossed out all her husband's personal belongings in the days after he died, essentially erasing him from the house. That complicated and impulsive decision on her part reverberated decades after his death.

I had given a few items away in the early months after your death, including a new wool navy blazer that you complained bitterly about wearing—"It's itchy!" you said—but you looked handsome in it and received so many compliments, you began to enjoy dressing up. Several of your teammates wore your blazer to their first communion services.

Many people advise not to rush, to try not to make significant sweeping changes too soon. For me, this was good advice, and thankfully both Dad and I agreed. But, after almost eight years, the room felt different to me. In the early days, I would cry on your bed. I could still smell you in your pillow. The red pom-pom on the hat of your favorite plushy stuffed snowman stayed crunchy from when you had chewed on it. But now the stuff felt more inanimate, not as infused with you as when you infused it with joy and care.

I looked around the room again and decided to dismantle your bed first. I sat on the floor with my coffee and phone and pulled two drawers full of jammies out from under your trundle bed. I emptied them onto the floor. I picked up each one and remembered you in them. I held them. I smelled them deeply to see if I could still smell you. I couldn't. Your terrycloth robe with the teddy bear ears was your favorite. You were so huggable in it—*my teddy bear*. I tied the arms of the robe around my neck like a scarf.

I pulled out a small, stapled book made of construction paper that was stuck in the back of one drawer. It was an old class project. I felt like I had discovered a lost treasure! I marveled at each page, looking at your handwriting, hurried as always, and your drawings. At the top of each page was a prompt: "My Favorite Toy" and "My Favorite Sport." You had answered every question with either the word soccer, or had drawn a soccer ball. "At least you were consistent," I said out loud and smiled. I felt you near and it warmed me. On the last page, the entry was "My Favorite Things," and you drew another soccer ball and wrote *Mom and Dad* with a blue heart. This melted me. Tears streamed down my face. *I miss you, Mack.* I lay down on the pile of your jammies and hugged as many as could fit in my arms and cried until I fell asleep.

At some point, my phone buzzed and woke me. Dad FaceTimed to check in, and when I answered with my puffy eyes and your teddy bear robe tied around my neck, he was mildly amused and concerned.

"Oh boy," he said.

"I'm okay," I assured him. "Just feeling the feels." It was getting dark, and I was on deadline. I brewed a fresh pot of decaf and gathered the boxes and green bags from the garage and headed back up.

After a slow start, I tore through the rest of your room like a tornado. I made three piles: save, give, throw away. In the pile to save: your soccer kits and gear. I also kept your teddy bear robe, slippers, and a pair of unopened Adidas socks. I still wear them when I run a 5K.

The biggest pile was to give away: lots of games, lightly used clothes, and stuffed animals. The whole furniture set and your bed we gave to a second cousin born several years after you died. His mom later sent us a video of him dancing around his new "big boy" room. His excitement breathed new life into the old Ethan Allen set that had also been your dad's.

And the last pile: to throw away. In your honor, I smiled as I opened the window and pulled up the screen to shove several large green plastic bags full of stuff through the window to thud on the porch below.

22

A Funeral, a Wedding, Graduations, and One Unwanted Guest

It has been six-and-a-half years since our Mack died suddenly on New Year's Eve 2012, just shy of his ninth birthday. We are always learning to live in new ways after our loss. We take it on as a part of life to discover how to carry Mack with us through life. As we entered the spring season of passages, including a funeral, a wedding, and a handful of graduations, I was surprised by my fatigue.

I have learned enough over the years to recognize when something is calling for my attention. In some ways, I think my body and soul knew before my brain. When I woke up on the Saturday after we returned home from our final trip, I arrived at my desk with my coffee and read and prayed and wrote in my journal to tap into my feelings, but something was stirring. Instead of setting off with my Saturday to-do list, I sat quietly to allow room for my spirit to speak to me. After an hour or so, the tears began flowing, and I couldn't turn them off. I let them come.

I entered a familiar room—a room of longing. A room whose door I open and peer into every day, but this day I allowed myself to fully enter and lament. Lament that Mack should've been at his grandfather's funeral to hear his dad preach a sermon that blew the doors off the church as he talked about how we live with death. Mack should've been at his cousin's wedding to dress up in a suit, complain about his leather shoes, and help us push his one-hundred-year-old great-grandmother around in her wheelchair. Yes, he should've been with us. Mack should've been here to wish his childhood friend well on her high school graduation. They had loved playing in the backyard, collecting and burying random objects and enjoying their own games. In the summer of 2012, Mack diligently hung a rope from our back deck with a small plastic bucket tied to the end. "It needs to stay there, Mom," he said to me earnestly, "in case she leaves me a note." It still dangles there, masked by a lilac tree.

And so, this morning, I sat on the hot coals of longing and memory and let them burn. It hurt. I cried cleansing tears. Because although it has been six-and-a-half years and we have learned to rearrange life around the amputation of Mack from our lives, his absence is a gaping hole nothing can replace. Nor should it.

I brewed another pot of coffee and gave myself time for the heat to subside and the grateful coolness to come.

And when it comes, I have found the healing balm is to act. These actions take various forms, but this time I went to the store and bought some fun gifts and cards on Mack's behalf to send to his friends with a note about how much they meant to Mack. My heart bursts with joy when I hear back from them and learn how much Mack still means to them.

The unwanted guest of grief is an ever-present shadow that demands our attention and acknowledgment. So be it. But we must also allow the love, memory, and joy of our loved ones to be celebrated and cherished, free from the shadows.

23

Merry Go Round and Round

While I was growing up, my mom made it a priority to take me and my siblings to the Smithsonian to visit the touring exhibits that came through the Washington, DC, museums. I am the eldest of four, and amid our collective moans and groans over another trek downtown from the suburbs in her diesel station wagon, my mom promised a ride or two on the lone carousel on the National Mall as a treat.

I loved the carousel. I remember when it was installed in 1981. We were delighted by what seemed a whimsical addition to the stately mall. A blue and orange striped circus-like tent top covered the elaborately decorated horses—years later, a sea dragon was added to the menagerie. A single-occupant ticket booth collected $1 per ride, and a food cart was stationed nearby. I remember sitting on a bench in the shade of a sweating, hot summer afternoon, munching on warm, salty popcorn while my younger brothers waved at me, my sister, and my mom each time the carousel circled in front of us.

Many years later, I sat on the same bench with C. We watched as Iz and Mack waved at us from the carousel and made funny faces to make us laugh. I smiled and waved, remembering my experience all those years ago. Like my mom, I had promised a ride on the carousel and a treat after we visited the Air and Space Museum. By then the carousel was weathered, charged $3.50 per ride, and was "adorably janky," as one reviewer aptly described it.

During a recent trip to the Smithsonian, I darted across the mall, avoiding puddles in between rain storms, to visit the carousel up close. It has permanently shut down, but it was still there, and had the air of a once-grand house surrounded by a black iron fence. The sea dragon, with teal blue scales and maniacal eyes, was always in high demand. I don't think my brothers, Mack, or Iz ever got to ride the dragon. I lingered behind the fence for a while and allowed the memories to burn through me.

Paint peeled from the horses, the sun had bleached the tent-like top, and the carousel had frozen in time. I realized that I, too, could have frozen. I often resented that time did not stop when time stopped for me. The relentless march of time, in and out of seasons, and through the calendar of holidays, comes round and round. It is unstoppable.

Slowly, tentatively, I climbed back on the merry-go-round of life. But I don't hesitate to give myself permission to hop off and buy some warm popcorn to munch while I sit on a bench to rest in the shade.

Part III

24

Kindling the Flame of Mack's Legacy

The first Mack Brady Soccer Clinic was quickly organized in January 2013 and coincided with Mack's birthday, January 16. And, each year since, we give a gift on his behalf in a random drawing to one boy and one girl at the clinic. Over the years, gifts have ranged from a soccer ball signed by the Penn State men and women players, to goalie gloves with the Mack Brady Memorial patch. This year, C had Mack patches embroidered on two black stocking caps.

In January 2023, we gathered for the eleventh annual Mack Brady Soccer Clinic hosted in the giant indoor field house, Holuba Hall, on Penn State University's campus. A record 206 youth soccer players came from clubs across the central Pennsylvania region to enjoy a free clinic with the Penn State men's and women's soccer teams. The vibe was electric. The kids love the college players. And the players love the kids.

The local State College Celtics club team, which started with Mack and his team twelve years ago, is now a large organization with more than two hundred members. They were there in force in their Celtic green kits with the Mack Brady Memorial patch on their sleeves in his honor. Most of the kids at the clinic weren't even born when Mack died in 2012, yet they speak of him and carry him on their sleeves so effortlessly. *Do you know how well you are loved, Mack?* I asked him. I watched soccer balls bounce helter-skelter while kids ran wild on another frigid January day.

Mack would love everything about this clinic.

Jeff Cook, the Penn State men's soccer coach, called the kids to gather around him and had them each sit on their soccer balls while he gave instructions for the ninety-minute clinic. The parents stood behind the kids and listened to Coach.

Mack's teammates started college this year, so most had returned to school, but their parents still came to the clinic as they have every year. My heart warms to stand with the moms. As I looked down the row at each of them, I was overwhelmed with gratitude for their friendship. Each of them carries their own losses, illnesses, and sufferings, yet they keep showing up to life. Showing up for all of us. Their courage gives me courage.

One of Mack's great friends, Quinn, now playing soccer for another school, was still home on winter break and came for the clinic. Quinn is tall and lean, with a ready smile—I imagine Mack would have a similar build.

"I think Mack would love this," I said to him. "It's really his legacy of friendship and fun, good soccer, on a snowy day."

"Oh, I think he would love it." Quinn smiled. "Mack would love it."

One of the most common questions both C and I have received from other bereaved parents is, "How will anyone remember my child lived?" I think establishing a legacy or a memorial is part of our continuing role as a parent that does not end with their death. Finding what feels right may take some trial and error, but allowing energy to flow instead of trying to stop it is beneficial. It seems to open some breathing room to give others space to honor someone they love, too.

Mack's best friend and teammate, John, and our neighbor Addie decided to honor Mack by raising funds for a permanent teepee to be added to the playground at their elementary school. I am not sure exactly what sparked it, but Mack had been constructing a teepee with random branches he collected in the yard throughout the fall of 2012. He darted outside after a storm to collect fallen branches and leaned them against a pine tree next to our house. I would watch from my desk as he dragged branches past my window to add to his growing structure. I shook my head and smiled at his latest project. He would laugh and say, "Don't mind me, ma'am!"

John had also constructed a teepee in his backyard, and he and Mack were working on another in a patch of trees on the school playground.

Fully supported by their parents and the school leadership, John and Addie spearheaded the initiative to fundraise, and the permanent teepee was constructed the following spring. John designed a sign that reads "Mack's Teepee. In celebration of a life lived in adventure."

Legacy can be foundations and policy initiatives created in response to the death of a child, often around the manner of their loss, such as sepsis awareness or pediatric cancer. Creating a legacy can be more intimate and personal, like starting a butterfly garden or contributing to a loved sport or event in your child's name.

What is most important is creating an opportunity to celebrate your child's life and remember his or her death. The way parents choose to honor their child will vary, of course, but creating opportunities each year around their birthday to remember their lives and speak their names invites space for others to share and remember them as well.

Jerry Sittser's book *A Grace Disguised: How the Soul Grows Through Loss* was one of the first books I read that helped me begin to understand my agency when everything else felt completely out of my control. Sittser wrote: "The experience of loss does not have to be the defining moment in our lives. . . . Instead, the defining moment can be our response to the loss. That response will largely determine the quality, the direction, and impact of our lives."[14]

Our response to their loss shapes their legacy.

25

Because Nothing Real Ever Dies

Mack loved our trip to the Netherlands in July 2012. We flew on Icelandair because it was cheap and a bit of an adventure. We sat two by two: Iz and me in front of C and Mack, both kids in the window seats. Mack, of course, had immediately charmed the flight attendants and was recognized as a "Junior Pilot." This meant special food, a lapel pin, playing cards, and a menagerie of goodies spread across his tray table. He was quite pleased with himself, and when I looked over my left shoulder between the seats, we smiled at one another. He shrugged as if to say, "What can I do? I'm awesome."

Many years later, as I looked into flights for C, Iz, and me, I looked again at Icelandair. A moment came to me from that trip in 2012, and I recalled that C and Iz had fallen asleep. I had looked over my left shoulder through the seats and Mack was awake. He smiled at me as I slid my hand through the seats, and we held fingers for a few minutes.

"I love you, sweet baby," I said out loud. "I miss you."

Memories of moments with Mack arrive unbidden at times. They live between us. I have come to understand that Mack has died, but he has not ceased to exist. I won't know exactly how this all works until my own death, but Mack is present to me in a myriad of ways. I think Mack carries his memories with him, as I have my own, and sometimes we enjoy a shared moment. I laugh out loud at these living snapshots because we always laughed together.

John O'Donohue, an Irish poet, theologian, and scholar of Meister Eckhart, the fourteenth-century German mystic, died suddenly in his sleep a few days after his fifty-second birthday in 2008. He wrote in *Anam Cara: A Book of Celtic Wisdom* that Meister Eckhart was once asked where a person's soul goes when it dies. I found this description helped me articulate what I was experiencing with Mack:

> *When the soul leaves the body, it is no longer under the burden and control of space and time. The soul is free; distance and separation hinder it no more. The dead are*

our nearest neighbors; they are all around us. Meister Eckhart was once asked, where does the soul of a person go when the person dies? He said, no place. Where else would the soul be going? Where else is the eternal world? It can be nowhere other than here. We have falsely spatialized the eternal world. We have driven the eternal out into some kind of distant galaxy. Yet, the eternal world does not seem to be a place but rather a different state of being. The soul of the person goes no place because there is no place else to go. The only difference between us and the dead is that they are now in invisible form. You cannot see them with the human eye. But you can sense the presence of those you love who have died. With the refinement of your soul, you can sense them. You feel that they are near.[15]

Yes. What relief to read this. What relief to be affirmed. I was regularly astounded by the vivid dreams, mystical moments, and dynamic experiences I've had over the years since Mack died. I did not dismiss these experiences or try to explain them away. Instinctively, I sensed that they were a comfort for me to receive, if I was willing to receive them. I held on to them. I wrote them down in my journal. And as I have written in other essays about the early mornings at my desk, I asked God to help me understand what was happening in my own life. I said out loud many times: "I am not imagining these things. I want to understand. I want to live the life I am having. I am not afraid. Help me!"

There were few people I could speak with about these experiences. I began reading online, following paths to blogs and books to educate myself. When I came across this quote from the medieval Benedictine nun Hildegard of Bingen (1098–1179), I felt affirmed to press on. Her quote is still taped to my desktop:

> *We cannot live in a world that is not our own, in a world that is interpreted for us by others. An interpreted world is not a home. Part of the terror is to take back our own listening, to use our own voice, to see our own light.*

My research and reading led me further back to a time when the death of loved ones was not easier but recognized and experienced as part of life. Closeness to our elderly relatives, closeness to birth, closeness to animals, all contributed to that shared experience. Our societal separation from animals, land, birth, and death has created an illusion of separateness from death. We find ourselves in a grief-illiterate society in the truest sense of the word—when death comes, we "have no words."

Our attitudes around death and dying have begun to change, and there are many resources to help us learn the language to express our experiences around grief and bereavement. Organizations like The Compassionate Friends, Open to Hope, Grief.com, Refuge in Grief, and other peer-to-peer support groups have stepped into this cultural gap and help to teach and support the bereaved.

In 2017, I attended my first Compassionate Friends national annual conference, where the bereaved come together to share through panels and seminars about how they have learned to live with the death of their children, siblings, and grandchildren.

Iz joined me in Orlando for the conference. She was nineteen at that time, but she was not ready to attend the sibling meetings, and felt that her best mental health boost would be to bob around the lazy river in a pink floatie with an umbrella-topped drink in hand. It would be another five years until Iz decided to see a counselor herself. As I walked back and forth to meetings, I could see her on the pool deck below and smiled. I was glad she was there with me.

One of the benefits of a large conference is there are small groups and break-out sessions specific to death passages: murder, suicide, vehicular manslaughter, long-term illness, sudden death, and many others. In my local group back home in Pennsylvania, we met as bereaved parents, regardless of the ages and circumstances of our children's deaths.

Some of the more popular sessions at this kind of conference have titles like "Signs from Heaven." I was amazed to join overflowing hotel ballrooms to hear people share about the myriad of ways they continue to hear from their deceased loved ones. It was affirming to learn that my experiences were quite common.

For some, signs are very direct, such as a dream, a vision, an angel, or, at times, a conversation. And for others, it is in the form of special reminders, like birds, butterflies, pennies, clouds, and feathers. It could be something intimate that you and your loved one shared.

Mack loved the character Acorn Tasha in *The Backyardigans*, a cartoon on Nick Jr. Acorn Tasha helped her friends, and she wore an acorn hat and a red sash with merit badges. Mack resonated with her character because he watched out for his friends, too. Mack collected acorns on our walks or at soccer practice, and would put them on top of his head to mimic Acorn Tasha and we'd laugh together. I continue to randomly discover perfectly formed acorn hats and I receive them as a gift from Mack.

An older gentleman came to a smaller breakout session and said, "I come to these sessions because I like to hear your stories, and I believe you. But I myself have never heard a thing from my son. Zilch." The other attendees clapped, and the session leader thanked him for his honesty.

The response of the session attendees affirmed that there is no right or wrong way to grieve. We each find our own way. I have received deep comfort from my "signs from heaven" and continuing connection with Mack. But I think of them as shooting stars of encouragement through the dark night. They can't do the work for me, or for any of us, but it's good to recognize them.

We Are Humans, Not Angels

Many mornings after Mack died, I would see my husband and daughter out of the house for work and school and then head up to Mack's room before I left for work. I would kneel at his bedside and hug his stuffed plush snowman and rub my fingers over the little red pom-pom hat that he had chewed—it stayed crunchy for a long time. I buried my face into his striped comforter to try to smell him.

One morning in late February 2013, I distinctly felt a presence behind my left shoulder and sensed a calming press on my back. It wasn't Mack; it was something else. I looked over my left shoulder and could see nothing, but I felt it. I lay my head down on Mack's bed to rest in the moment.

This experience sent me on a new journey. I was raised in the Episcopal church, so the notion of angels and assigned guardian angels was new to me. It didn't take long for me to find many spine-tingling accounts of angelic intervention in human lives.

I came across a book by Billy Graham, first published in 1975, called *Angels: Ringing Assurance that We Are Not Alone*, where Graham shares stories of angelic intervention in human life. Graham decided to write the book himself to help reclaim the role of angels that make prominent and consistent appearances throughout the Bible. It reminded me of similar stories I heard when I was in Burkina Faso. Graham wrote:

> *I am convinced that these heavenly beings exist and that they provide unseen aid on our behalf. The Bible teaches that angels intervene in the affairs of nations. They guide, comfort, and provide for the people of God in the midst of suffering and persecution. Believers, look up—take courage. The angels are nearer than you think.*[16]

After Mack died, we received many encouraging notes about how he had become an angel and earned his wings in heaven. Of course, we received them as the comfort they were intended to be, but our humanness is actually to be cherished:

God has created beings that are heavenly bodies
and beings that are earthly.

We are earthly beings. We are distinctly
human and mutually linked to the earth. *From
dust you came, and to dust you will return*—we are
reminded of our mortality in every Ash Wednes-
day service. In fact, our bodies return to nurture
the earth after we die. But after death, we don't
become something else; instead, we emerge into
an "imperishable" body as described by Paul in
I Corinthians. We will be recognizable as our
unique selves.

We are spirit and matter. And our matter,
matters.

How connected we are to the earth, how
outrageously unsubtly our humanity mirrors the
ripening, birth, and death of the living things
with whom we share life on earth. Hildegard of
Bingen mused that, like the earth, women are
born with all their seeds tucked inside. It is not
whether these seeds are fertilized or come into
fruition that define us, but rather that they are
there.

But God created heavenly bodies for a different purpose. The Oxford English Dictionary defines an angel as "a member of a class of celestial

beings considered intermediate between God and humanity and typically acting as attendants, messengers, or agents of God."[17]

In my reading, I came across a book written by Lillie Leonardi called *In the Shadow of a Badge* published in 2013. Leonardi was one of the first responders to the scene of Flight 93 on 9/11 in Shanksville, Pennsylvania. At that time, she was a community outreach liaison officer for the FBI and described the scene at the crash site:

> *On the field, the shimmer of light began to grow off to my left until it was almost blinding. I turned and looked at it more directly, and it began to evolve into a foggy white mist. The white mist then began to move, swirling in patterns of spectacular white light. Then, before my eyes, the mist took shape. To my amazement, there at the left of the crash site stood what appeared to be a legion of angels. There were hundreds of them standing in columns—a field of angels emerging from the realms of the mist. I recognized them as archangels with their wings arched up toward the sky.*[18]

Leonardi kept her vision to herself for some time for fear her colleagues would think she was having a mental breakdown. But she eventually shared her experience to offer comfort to the surviving family members.

When I read these stories, I ponder the visible world as a keyhole to the vast invisible. At times of great mourning, on a national level or in our personal lives, I think we glimpse the invisible vastness for our comfort and hope.

27

The Interior Garden

In my buffet of reading across the Christian denominational spectrum, I was comforted to learn that the contemplative writers of old and those teaching us today have largely the same message.

"Life is an inside job," wrote Anne Lamott in *Almost Everything: Notes on Hope* in 2018.

And from St. Isaac the Syrian, Bishop of Ninevah, who lived from 640–700, whose teaching on prayer echoes across the centuries:

Be at peace with your own soul,
then heaven and earth
Will be at peace with you.

Enter eagerly into the treasure house
That is within you,
You will see things that are in heaven;
For there is but one single entry
To them both.

The ladder that leads to the Kingdom
Is hidden within your soul . . .

Dive into yourself,
And in your soul you will discover
The stairs by which to ascend.

And another from St. Teresa of Àvila, who lived and served from 1515–1582: "The path to God leads us on a journey of self-discovery. To know the self is to know God." That is no small task. It is humbling. In fact, it is the work of life for each of us. No one is off the hook. And no one can do it for you.

A series of podcasts called "Turning to the Mystics," hosted by James Finley at the Center for Action and Contemplation (CAC), introduced me to Teresa of Àvila. A Spanish Carmelite nun and author of *The Interior Castle*, St. Teresa also mentored the Carmelite friar St. John of the Cross (1542–1591), who wrote the classic *Dark Night of the Soul*.

St. Teresa used the castle as a familiar metaphor to describe the interior journey and contemplative prayer practices as a guide for her fellow sisters. Later, she evolved the metaphor from a firm structure to a garden to better capture the organic, unending, and unfolding interior life.

I have shared in earlier essays that my morning practice of reading, praying, and journaling had become a habit long before Mack was born. But after Mack died, my need deepened.

After years of reflective prayer, writing, and typing endless lists of prayer concerns for myself and other people, I felt nudged to put my mechanical pencil down. To stop typing. To listen. To open myself. To receive.

Unfortunately, I did not discover a secret garden beautifully manicured, bursting in bloom, and intact, with a bench installed for my contemplative moments. Instead, it was more like a plot. A plot that every human inherits as a mark of and connection with God, our Creator. A plot that cannot be trespassed or taken from us by any other human. A plot that waits patiently for our daily attention and care.

There are many brambles and vines to wrestle. Each represents specific people and events in life that have hurt us. There are people we have hurt. And there are prickly thorns in ourselves that need constant pruning. It is a practice without end, full of discovery and delight, requiring regular forgiveness and gentleness with ourselves and others. But by tending and tilling this space within us, we create the compost of our lives. We take ownership of our whole selves: our failings, our deep sufferings, and our gifts. We enliven the ground, which allows us to receive newness of life.

Ruth Burrows, the pen name for Rachel Gregory, was a contemporary Carmelite nun and served in the same tradition as St. Teresa, but on the windswept northeast coast in Norfolk, England, until her death in 2023. She wrote several bestselling books on the Christian life. I read *The Interior Castle Explored*, Burrows's commentary on St. Teresa's work. And I recently read *Love Unknown*, which Burrows was commissioned to write for the Archbishop of Canterbury's Lent Book in 2012.

In *Love Unknown*, Burrows shares this reflection:

> There is a ruling insight that covers and controls my life and all that I would or could communicate to others. It runs through everything I have written: God offers himself in total love to each one of

us. Our part is to open our hearts to re-
ceive this gift . . . We think we must first
save ourselves, perfect ourselves, and then
offer ourselves to Love. No! Only love can
save, purify, and cause us to expand and
expand to receive more and more. This we
learn from Jesus, for, as Julian of Norwich
clearly perceived, where Jesus is there is the
Trinity.

Oh, how difficult it is to truly believe I am
loved and beloved. How hard it is for each of us
to truly believe in the goodness of God in the
midst of endless suffering, not only in our own
lives, but in our world. That Jesus was God in
human form who came to help release us from
burdensome and unnecessary human rules, to
assure us of his love for each one of us. To die for
us. Then to rise again to defeat death itself. How
thick the brambles grow and distort Jesus's own
words.

I returned to Hildegard's challenge taped to
my desktop:

We cannot live in a world that is not our
own, in a world that is interpreted for us

*by others. An interpreted world is not a
home. Part of the terror is to take back our
own listening, to use our own voice, to see
our own light.*

I realized there were many areas of my life
that I allowed to be interpreted for me. I needed
to take back my light. I pressed on reading, praying, and allowing for newness.

Burrows wrote, "I know no writer who has
so conveyed to us the tender, incredible nearness
of our Lord to us" as Julian of Norwich (1343-
1416) described:

*Highest and mightiest, noblest and wor-
thiest, is lowest and meekest, homeliest and
most courteous. For our soul is so preciously
loved that is highest, that it overpasseth the
knowing of all creatures: that is to say, there
is no creature that is made that may more
fully know how much and how sweetly
and how tenderly our Maker loveth us.*

There is another contemporary American
woman whose voice has emerged through the
babel as clear as a bell. I hear echoes of the same

passion and sentiment toward Jesus that Julian of Norwich expressed in the 1300s. I am struck by the similarity of their language, centuries apart, describing Jesus. I press on to learn from both women.

Beth Moore, a Bible teacher and author of more than twenty books, including a recently released bestselling memoir, *All My Knotted-Up Life,* has uncommon courage. After a lifetime of service, she left her own denomination and, through the unending mystery and, might I add, good humor of the Holy Spirit, who blows its seeds where and how it chooses, Moore is now worshipping and teaching at an Anglican church in Houston, Texas.

Moore challenges each of us, in the spirit of Hildegard, and echoing the words of Julian of Norwich, to read the Bible ourselves. Moore challenges us to release the burden of human rules and interpretations that keep us entangled, and to allow ourselves to be known and loved by God.

I came knocking each morning, looking for Mack. And Mack is there, beloved, whole, and free. What I am learning to receive is that God was looking for me, and looks for each one of us, in the most tender and courteous way.

28

Tender Care of My Earthly Body

In the gym where I work out, the lights are orange. The effect of the dim light softens the view of one another, but more importantly, my own body when I catch sight of myself in the mirrors. The music blares. There is a buzz of energy. The smell of sweat. I don't know the people I see regularly, but we smile and say hello and comment on each other's footwear.

I have often mused to myself that the gym is not unlike the dive bars of my college days. My friends and I would head out to the packed bar, overly groomed, where the lights were dim and the music blared. I saw the same people regularly, although I did not know them, but we would say hello and comment on each other's footwear.

When AC/DC's "Back in Black" comes on, it flings open a door of memories and I am transported to Thirsty Thursdays, drinking cheap beer and smoking Marlboro Lights. I surprise myself by recalling the lyrics. My pace quickens with the first sip of memory, and I sing out loud to the amusement of those on the treadmills on either side of me. Then, we segue into a hip-hop song that shifts us into the present. My pace slows, and I linger in the dusty rooms of memory.

I remember several of my drinking buddies. We were the ones who couldn't stop drinking when the bar closed at 2 A.M. and went on to "after parties" when the others went home. I recall those who have since died; a few of suicide, others from the exhausted minds and bodies of addiction. I remember each of them by name. My cheeks prickle, flushed with the harsh truth from F. Scott Fitzgerald: "First you take a drink, then the drink takes a drink, then the drink takes you."

After exhausting my relationships, body, and mind, I stopped drinking and smoking at twenty-three. I smoked my last pack of Marlboro Lights on an extended layover at Charles De Gaulle Airport in Paris en route to West Africa, where I spent a year as a short-term missionary. I lived on a mission compound alone in a mud brick house where the generator shut off every night at 10 P.M., leaving me blinking into the dark nights of utter silence and solitude. I was forever changed by that undeserved gift: a year of quiet healing and sobriety mentored by two of the most gentle and faithful people I have ever met.

The practices of mind and body I began in Burkina Faso endured for more than two decades. In the mornings after Mack's death, I returned to my desk in the early hours, knowing instinctively that it was a sacred space. But I was exhausted to the core. It took every ounce of me to maintain my family, home, work, and the new part of my life as a bereaved mom.

When I arrived at my desk, I was unsettled. Unsettled because the gaping rip of Mack's death opened other wounds long buried. I was surprised by this; it was unexpected. I was reminded of the song "Anthem" by Leonard Cohen from his 1992 album *The Future*. Its chorus has made its way onto greeting cards and bumper stickers: "There is a crack, a crack in everything. That's how the light gets in."

This is true. But unless the pot is empty, there is a serious amount of stuff that oozes out of that crack first. Mack's death cracked open the pot, and the gunk inside demanded my attention.

An old friend beckoned to me for respite. I began drinking a glass of red on weekend evenings, finding it dimmed the chatter inside me and served as a welcomed distraction from the unfolding new life I had not chosen. Over several years, the weekend extended to a glass every night, and I realized that my old needy friend had moved back into my life and rearranged the furniture to suit itself.

In June 2020, during the height of the pandemic, I arrived at my desk and looked at my tired reflection in the window and cried.

"You are no friend to me," I said out loud. To wine. To myself.

The old frenemy overshadowed the practices in my life that most nourished me: a clarity of mind in the morning to read, pray, and write. An energy in my body to exercise, eat, and sleep well.

I turned to reading a genre called "Quit Lit." Two books were enlightening to me. Annie Grace's *This Naked Mind* and Laura McKowen's *We Are the Luckiest* helped me shift from the dual thinking of, *do I have a drinking problem?* to the more nuanced question, *what is my relationship with alcohol?*

By shifting my thinking, I opened a conversation with myself and reflected more critically, eventually acknowledging the few benefits drinking had provided throughout my life. Again, I stopped drinking. I determined to be fully present in my life, in my mind, in my body, and fully awake to hear the gentle teachings and whispers to my soul.

In James Finley's book *The Healing Path* and his series of podcasts, "Turning to the Mystics" on the Center for Action and Contemplation website (cac.org), he emphasized that "nothing real ever dies." It was a welcoming thought to me in relation to Mack, cultivating our continuing bonds beyond his death. What I was not prepared for was that this truth was not siloed to Mack. It is the truth of all lives: nothing real ever dies, the good nor the bad.

Finley counsels that in the regular practice of our quiet time or rendezvous with God in solitude, we may eventually be nudged to undergo a "fearless inventory." A fearless inventory means that the hastily buried or stitched-over events and relationships in our lives, done to us and done by us, come undone. Issues that have been quietly waiting in the soil of our lives for the opening, the light, sprout and ask for our attention. It may be that we are pricked in an area of our lives that needs special care. It could be in our relationship with food, money, alcohol, or another person. This is terrifying. It is humbling. And this is when it is easy to run through the garden of our lives, dumping soil and mulch to bury it all again, grab a glass of wine, an epic Netflix series, an on-line shopping spree, CrossFit, volunteer service, work—you name it—and distract ourselves from working the soil of our own lives.

I spent many mornings sitting at my desk in the pre-dawn hours, asking God to help me enter my own life. I know now that I didn't fully realize what I was asking for. I was interested in Mack. God was interested in the whole of me.

Nadia Bolz-Weber wrote in a 2022 blog on human bodies, "All this is to say, that God saves you IN your body, not FROM your body. Your body is in the same form and substance as that which God chose to put on and walk among us as Jesus. Your body is holy and beautiful to God— your young, old, fit, fat, cis, queer, disabled, strong body. For after all, it is the human body in which God placed God's image, the *image dei*."[19]

The inner practices of solitude, prayer, meditation, mindfulness, and self-talk are known to us, but like exercise, it takes determination and discipline to make them a habit in our daily lives. The inner life is a spacious and unknown frontier, and entering that space is overwhelming the first time. It is a crowded place with many voices and memories competing for our attention. We need good teachers and guides to help us.

Ruth Burrows, the pen name for Rachel Gregory, a Carmelite nun in Norfolk, England, wrote bestselling books on contemplative prayer throughout her life, spanning one hundred years. In *Extravagent Love*, published in 2022, Burrows wrote that after a lifetime of ministry, there is a secret pain that too few speak about and fewer can articulate to ourselves, much less to God. Burrows writes:

> *It is an incommunicable pain having to do with me just being me and a me I do not like. Instinctively we contrast this unclaimed pain with "real" suffering: bereavement, oppression, torture, hunger, imprisonment, illness, and so on, and we feel still more ashamed and self-despising. Some of us*

> *know this about ourselves but some, I think,*
> *do not and therefore this particular pain,*
> *so precious, I believe, in God's eyes, is not*
> *exposed to him and so it blocks our capacity*
> *for wholehearted love; we are that much less*
> *a person. The pain may be precisely the in-*
> *ability to accept self. Let us take every aspect*
> *of our human experience and spread it out*
> *to God without fear, without shame.*

There is no area untouchable to God. By getting our hands in the dirt of ourselves, we prepare our soil to receive the gifts of forgiveness and compassion offered to each of us, in abundance. God works on compassion in our souls. And as this slow acceptance of our whole, naked, imperfect self grows, it is extended out as if through a prism to others.

This is not a "one and done" moment. It is the daily care of our whole selves in relationship to body, mind, spirit, and those among us, throughout our remaining lives. This quotidian, or dailyness of living, is radically reflected in all of Creation that we share as created beings.

A song from the Lumineers 2012 album *Ho, Hey!* brings me back into the moment. I smile and sing the chorus. I sang it to Mack many times and he would play-faint onto the couch.

The class ends with *two claps on three!* I dab my ever-sweaty menopausal body with a towel and shake my blender bottle before taking a sip. The shot of apple cider vinegar I had added to my water for a little extra boost before leaving home had settled on the bottom.

"I like your shoes," I say to the woman next to me. I do not know her, but I see her regularly.

"Thanks." She smiles and leans toward me. "I like AC/DC, too."

29

The Search for Meaning in
a #Blessed Culture

When I returned from West Africa at twenty-three years old, I could not stop talking about living in the bush. It was such a transformative time for me, I managed to weave it into every conversation to the point that my family began teasingly asking (and still do), "Wait, did you go to Africa?"

It wasn't until I began working for an international charity where most of my colleagues had lived, worked, and continued to travel across the African continent that I could put my experience into a healthier perspective. I was surrounded by people who were moved by their hands-on work and by the gracious people they encountered, and were at times disheartened by the endlessness of the need.

After Mack died, I felt a similar disconnect when few people around me had any context by which to understand what I was going through. I needed to find people who wanted to talk about the dynamic, spiritual, painful, and astounding things I was experiencing without being uncomfortable. I found this tribe of people in my reading and among other bereaved parents.

We lived in a small college town with no Compassionate Friends chapter, but we did have a local nonprofit created to support children and teens in grief. The kids and families met for pizza as a large group and then broke into smaller sessions for specific ages. That is when the parents met.

Many Thursdays over the years, I left campus just in time to gather with the other parents. I never regretted being there. Some were caretakers of their grandchildren, some had stillborn children and brought their older kids for support, and some of us had young children who died, and we came on our own. Finding a safe space to share with a group of other bereaved parents is like finding people who speak English in a foreign country. It soothes your ears.

In these meetings, I learned practical ideas about how to handle holidays and enjoyed hearing how other people remembered their children. Sometimes we talked about dreams and visions;

other times we spoke about what we do with our loved ones' "stuff," which is always tricky. The point is that there is no one path, just as there is no "correct" path for marriage, parenting, or any other great journeys of our lives. We listen, encourage, share, learn, and then figure out what works for us.

It was in this space, too, that I realized how many people often felt lonely and isolated in a culture, and sometimes within their own families, that do not want to talk about death. That group became a refuge, a singular space to speak freely and openly about their deceased children.

A few years after Mack died, a woman said to me, "It makes me feel bad when I think of you and Mack because I am so blessed."

Her comment cuts to the heart of a cultural myth that persists as strongly in the church as it does in popular culture: illness, death, job loss, addiction, essentially the challenges of most every human life, are seen as sad events that derail us from the #blessed state.

This is why we are collectively baffled when seemingly "successful" people die of suicide. "Why?" we wonder, when they have everything we've been told make a meaningful life.

Rowan Williams, the Welsh Anglican bishop and former Archbishop of Canterbury, calls this the "myth of self-sufficiency." When life happens beyond our control, we are essentially awakened from the illusion of control. Williams writes, "Once we have been healed from that lethal wound that has broken our connection with living truth, healed from the terrible fiction that freedom is separation rather than communion, the world is made new.[20]

It is fear and shame that lead us to silo portions of ourselves and experiences into containers of bad and good. But wholeness emerges when embracing all of ourselves. Empty out the silos to allow the rich compost of our lives. The labels of bad and good don't work. The better question is whether we have allowed our whole selves, our whole messy lives, to be redeemed.

Over the years I have read everything I could find to help enlighten my experience. I wanted to be around people who were not afraid to speak about death, and in finding them, I realized again, as I had done after returning from Africa, that I was not alone.

British mystic Caryll Houselander, who ministered to many suffering people after World War

II, wrote: "We cannot give a cure, we can give sympathy . . . and this means sharing in another's sorrow, a real self-giving. Anything else can be given without involving self, but sympathy *is* giving self."[21]

In the quiet after-hours of school libraries and online support groups, armies of the bereaved gather together to share of themselves and encourage the endless flow of soldiers to the ranks. They are largely invisible until you meet death, and then suddenly you find you are surrounded by these warriors of life who give endlessly because of, and not in spite of, their loves and losses.

30

"God, Help Me Do What is Mine to Do"

If you have flipped to this final chapter of the book, as I did many times in my reading, to find out if you will survive, the short answer is, you won't like it, life will never be the same, but it can be good. The choice to survive is truly yours, but it is yours, and that is empowering.

In Nicholas Wolterstorff's *Lament for a Son*, he reflected on the passage of time after the death of his twenty-five-year-old son Eric in 1983:

> *Rather often I am asked whether the grief remains as intense as when I wrote. The answer is, No. The wound is no longer raw. But, it has not disappeared. That is as it should be. If he was worth loving, he is worth grieving over. . . . Grief is existential testimony to the worth of the one loved. That worth abides. So, I own my grief. I do not try to put it behind me, to*

> *get over it, to forget it . . . Every lament is*
> *a love-song.*[22]

As I approach the twelfth year of life beyond Mack's death, I still fill my coffee in a glass mug each morning and sit at my desk to rendezvous in the spaciousness of the quiet hours. I am surrounded by my books, journal, Bible, photos, and icons. Sticky notes full of quotes and the titles of more books to be read fill my monitor. And, I have a modern *memento mori* in the form of a brightly colored skull planter with a succulent.

Soon after Mack died, I knew I would find him in this space, and I have. It is a journey of endless discovery.

"If we do not transform our pain, we will most assuredly transmit it," wrote Richard Rohr.[23] And that is the hard but necessary daily work of ownership that each of us must take on ourselves.

The dailiness of life is just as necessary in our physical lives as in our spiritual lives. Just as I need to attend to the daily and unending care and keeping of my body, people, home, job, pets, and plants, I have an unending need for connection, prayer, scripture reading, and reminders each morning that I am loved by God.

In this space, I come to lament, as love-song, in memories, tears, and laughter, to face the truth of Mack's absence and presence in my life. Mack still *is*. My time here is not done. Our story is not yet finished.

I wish I could tell you there is a quota in life for suffering, but I don't think there is. Loved ones continue to be born and die, people get sick, there are weddings and graduations, relationships fall apart, and some are renewed.

In short: life continues in all of its beauty and terror. But maybe I am a little less afraid.

Within all of this, we can only control our response. It is our great power, our only power. "God spares us from nothing, while unexplainably sustaining us in all things," James Finley wrote in *The Healing Path*.

One of the yellow stickies on my monitor is a quote from St. Francis of Assisi, and I say it out loud each morning as I wrap up my journal and prayers:

"God, help me do what is mine to do."

And I wish the same for you.

Notes

1. Littlefield, Bill. "Grieving Family Finds Joy - and Healing - in Soccer," aired on *Only A Game*, WBUR, 23 June 2017, www.wbur.org/onlyagame/2017/06/23/goalkeeper-penn-state-soccer-brady. Transcript reprinted with permission from Victor Hernandez, Chief Content Officer, WBUR.

2. Elizabeth Lesser, *Broken Open: How Difficult Times Can Help Us Grow* (New York: Penguin Random House, 2005).

3. Martha Whitmore Hickman, *Healing After Loss: Daily Meditations for Working Through Grief* (New York: William Morrow, 1994), January 15 entry.

4. Sandy Fox, *Creating a New Normal . . . After the Death of a Child* (Bloomington: iUniverse Inc., 2010), 58.

5. Katherine Mansfield, *Katherine Mansfield's Letters to John Middleton Murry, 1913–1922*, 1st American ed. (New York: Alfred A. Knopf, 1951), 616.

6. Anne Morrow Lindbergh, Hour of Gold, Hour of Lead: Diaries and Letters of Anne Morrow Lindbergh, 1929-1932 (Harcourt Brace Jovanovich, 1973), 214–215.

7. Anne Lamott, *Traveling Mercies: Some Thoughts on Faith* (New York: Pantheon, 1999), 72.

8. John O'Donohue, "The Absent Threshold: The Paradox of Divine Knowing in Meister Eckhart," *Eckhart Review* 12, no. 1 (April 2015), 22.

9. Henri J. M. Nouwen, Bread for the Journey: A Daybook of Wisdom and Faith (San Francisco: HarperOne, 1997), August 29 entry, 278.

10. Samara Quintero and Jamie Long, "Toxic Positivity: The Dark Side of Positive Vibes," accessed August 14, 2024, https://thepsychologygroup.com/toxic-positivity.

11. Alan Wolfelt, "Educational Seminars for Bereavement Caregivers," accessed August 14, 2024, https://www.centerforloss.com/wp-content/uploads/2023/10/TrainingCatalog_20242025_Web.pdf.

12. Dietrich Bonhoeffer, *Letters and Papers from Prison*, ed. Eberhard Bethge (Macmillan, 1972), 176-177.

13. Henri J. M. Nouwen, *Bread for the Journey: A Daybook of Wisdom and Faith* (New York: HarperCollins, 1997), May 10 entry, 161.

14. Jerry Lawson Sittser, *A Grace Disguised: How the Soul Grows through Loss*. Expanded ed. (Grand Rapids: Zondervan, 2006), 18.

15. John O'Donohue, *Anam Cara: A Book of Celtic Wisdom* (New York: HarperCollins, 1997), 226.

16. Billy Graham, *Angels: Ringing Assurance that We Are Not Alone* (Nashville: Thomas Nelson, 2011), 24.

17. *Oxford English Dictionary*, Revised 2019, s.v. "angel," accessed August 14, 2024, https://www.oed.com/dictionary/angel_n?tl=true.

18. Lillie Leonardi, *In the Shadow of a Badge: A Memoir about Flight 93, a Field of Angels, and My Spiritual Homecoming* (New York: Hay House, 2013), 38.

19. Nadia Bolz-Weber, "Human Bodies and the Image of God: A Sermon on Shame and Healing," *The Corners* (August 22, 2022), https://thecorners.substack.com/p/human-bodies-and-the-image-of-god.

20. Rowan Williams, "Heaven Meets Earth," *Plough Quarterly*, 38 (Winter 2024), 61.

21. Masie Ward, *Caryll Houselander: Divine Eccentric* (Providence: Cluny, 2021), 259.

22. Nicholas Wolterstorff, *Lament for a Son* (Grand Rapids: Eerdmans Publishing Company, 1987), 5.

23. Richard Rohr, "Transforming Pain," accessed August 15, 2024, https://cac.org/daily-meditations/transforming-pain-2018-10-17/.

Resources

We live in a grief-illiterate society. After the death of a child, we often hear, "there are no words." But there are words. Peer-to-peer support groups, like the ones listed below, welcome the newly bereaved into communities that support and educate in a disorienting new world. Each of us is unique, and it takes time to discover the communities that resonate best with you.

• *Center for Loss & Life Transition* was founded by Dr. Alan Wolfelt. centerforloss.com

• *Compassionate Friends* is a national peer-to-peer organization dedicated to supporting families after a child dies. They have strong parent, grandparent, and sibling programs. On their website, you will find articles, resources to locate local support groups, annual conference details, and Facebook communities. compassionatefriends.org

• *Evermore* was founded by Joyal Mulheron, a bereaved mom and lawyer, to advocate for bereavement policies and practices to support families after the death of a loved one. evermore.org

• *Everything Happens* is Kate Bowler's website, named after her 2017 book, *Everything Happens for a Reason: And Other Lies I've Loved.* Her book opened a conversation within the Christian community about the myths of suffering and loss. Kate continues this conversation with subsequent books, a podcast, and resources on katebowler.com

• *Grief.com* is a resource for all types of loss "because love never dies." David Kessler is the founder and provides articles, books, and opportunities for continuing education for both counselors and peer support groups. grief.com

• *Open to Hope* is a multimedia website with articles and podcasts that cover all types of loss. Drs. Gloria and Heidi Horsley host a weekly podcast that covers the ripple effects of grief in our lives. opentohope.com

• *Refuge in Grief* is the online community created by Megan Devine for "grief support that doesn't suck." Her book *It's OK That You're Not OK* has helped to update the tired language and experience of grief and loss for a new generation. refugeingrief.com

• *Speaking Grief* is a public media initiative, produced by Lindsey Whissel Fenton, aimed at creating a more grief-aware society by validating the experience of grievers and helping to guide those who wish to support them. speakinggrief.org

Further Reading

Bingen, Hildegard of, *Scivias*, 1990.

Bolz-Weber, Nadia, *Pastrix: The Cranky, Beautiful Faith of a Sinner & Saint*, 2013.

Bowler, Kate, *Everything Happens for a Reason: And Other Lies I've Loved*, 2017.

Burrows OCD, Ruth, *Interior Castle Explored: St Teresa's teaching on the Life of Deep Union with God*, 2007.

Burrows OCD, Ruth, *Extravagant Love*, 2022.

Campbell, Colin, *Finding the Words: Working Through Profound Loss with Hope and Purpose*, 2023.

Chittister OBE, Joan, *Scarred by Struggle, Transformed by Hope*, 2005.

Finley, James, *The Healing Path*, 2023.

Grace, Annie, *This Naked Mind: Control Alcohol, Find Freedom, Discover Happiness & Change Your Life*, 2018.

Hickman, Martha Whitmore, *Healing After Loss*, 1994.

Lesser, Elizabeth, B*roken Open: How Difficult Times Can Help Us Grow*, 2005.

McGinn, Bernard, *The Foundations of Mysticism: Origins to the Fifth Century*, 1991.

McKowen, Laura, *We Are the Luckiest: The Surprising Magic of a Sober Life*, 2020.

Moore, Beth, *All My Knotted-Up Life: A Memoir*, 2023.

Nouwen, Henri, *Bread for the Journey: A Daybook of Wisdom and Faith*, 1997.

Pizzuto, Vincent, *Contemplating Christ: The Gospels and the Interior Life*, 2018.

Rast, David Steindl, Grateful.org.

Riley, Cole Arthur, *This Here Flesh: Spirituality, Liberation, and the Stories that Make Us*, 2022.

Rilke, Rainer Marie, *The Dark Interval: Letters on Loss, Grief, and Transformation*, 2018.

Rohr, Richard, *Falling Upward*, 2nd edition, 2023.

Rutledge, Fleming, *Advent: The Once and Future Coming of Jesus Christ*, 2018.

About the Author

Elizabeth's son, Mack, died suddenly of sepsis on New Year's Eve 2012. In the aftermath, she began reading widely from other bereaved parents to learn how they lived beyond the death of a beloved child. As many of us discover, sharing our stories helps illuminate the path, but we each must learn to walk them ourselves.

Elizabeth teaches at Penn State University and her essays can be read on Motherwell, Modern Loss, Open to Hope, and Compassionate Friends. She has participated in several national Compassionate Friends conferences and served on the content advisory board for the documentary *Speaking Grief* that seeks to help us all get better at grief. Elizabeth and her family founded the Mack Brady Memorial Soccer Fund at Penn State in Mack's honor.